Treasures of the British Museum

TREASURES OF THE

This book is based on the Thames Television series
of the same name, and its distinguished authors are
contributors to that series. Thames extends its thanks
to them, and to Sir John Wolfenden and the Trustees
and Keepers of the British Museum for their help.
The opinions and statements contained in the book
remain those of the individual authors. Thames wishes
also to acknowledge the valuable assistance
given by Dr Barry Turner in its preparation.

BRITISH MUSEUM

With an Introduction by Sir John Wolfenden

Collins   St James's Place, London

William Collins Sons & Co Ltd
London · Glasgow · Sydney · Auckland
Toronto · Johannesburg

First published 1971
© Thames Television 1971

ISBN 0 00 211834 3

Set in Monophoto Poliphilus
Made and printed in Great Britain by
Jarrold and Sons Ltd, Norwich

Contents

Introduction

The British Museum

John Wolfenden

I would not claim that the British Museum was unique among the museums and galleries of the world. That would be presumptuous and very un-British. But I do claim that it is, at least, unusual.

The ground for that claim is clear enough. When Parliament decided, in 1753, to grant funds for the purchase of the collections of Sir Hans Sloane and the Harleian manuscripts, the nation became the owners of a remarkable congeries of objects, antiquarian, historical, scientific, and of reading matter, written, printed, ancient and modern. And ever since then this double nature of the British Museum has persisted. True, the natural history collections were 'hived off' to South Kensington in 1881 and became a separate institution as a result of the British Museum Act of 1963. But apart from this wholly reasonable secession, which the parent took in her enlightened stride, the British Museum in Bloomsbury has continued to live a double life. We are not either a museum or a library. We are both.

No other museum in the world, so far as I know, has within its walls its country's national library of research and reference (containing six or seven million volumes). No other museum receives by law a copy of every item published within its national boundaries – to an extent, which, in our case, demands two-thirds of a mile of shelving every year. No other museum contains documents comparable with the *Codex Sinaiticus* or the Lindisfarne Gospels. Conversely, so far as I know, no national library has within its walls major collections of Assyrian, Egyptian, Greek, Roman and medieval objects, or of clocks or of Javanese puppets. In short, we have the responsibility of being in world class (or in the international league) both as a museum and as a library. This is not a boast; it is a simple statement of historical fact and present responsibility.

But there is a unifying thread. This double nature may have been wished on us two hundred and more years ago by the accident of the nature of the collections which were then acquired. But consistent practice over those two centuries has developed the accident into a policy, the fortuitous into a principle.

There are two sides to this, one of theory and one of practice; and as is right in any coherent situation, each justifies the other. The theory validates the practice and the practice proves the theory.

The basis of the theory is simply the unity of knowledge. Right from the earliest days of human speculation and inquiry down to the times of Sir Hans Sloane, knowledge was regarded as one interconnected unity. Diversity certainly there was, but an underlying unity was assumed. Aristotle, to take a familiar example, was at the same time a metaphysical and moral philosopher and a collector of everything from political constitutions to animals and plants. And so were his predecessors in the Middle East and his successors in Western Europe. It is not that he was separately a specialist metaphysician and a specialist natural scientist and then miraculously joined the two specialisms together. The two activities were not separated. That was the general background of intellectual activity until very lately, and there are still the vestiges of it in those universities which engagingly describe as Natural Philosophy what the rest of us call Physics.

It is almost within living memory that bits of this unity were snipped off, tied up in neat parcels and given distinctive specialist names. It may well be that this was, in its day, desirable or at any rate necessary. So much more was being found out, in an incredibly short space of time, that the unity could not, from the sheer weight of new information, be held together. Especially was this so in the natural sciences, where we now have divisions and subdivisions into what might naughtily be called 'microscopic' detail. Clearly, this specialization was necessary for the pursuit of detailed knowledge and without it the scientific advances of the past century could not have been made. So the polymath went out of fashion, even out of existence. Or if he did occur it was by joining specialisms together in his own thinking and experience, not by moving outwards from a basic unity.

Today there is a swing back, a search for unifying principles, a desire for something which will transcend the obvious diversities and specialisms. The increase in inter-disciplinary studies is a symptom, the attempt to synthesize as well as to discriminate. This is not an attempt to reach the kind of unity which is a blank, dull, null, amorphous sameness or an overriding of distinctions. The unity is rich and diverse, living and, ideally, comprehensive, each element in it illustrating and illuminating all the others, so that each is the more intelligible and appreciable for the presence of the rest.

Does all this seem a very long way from the British Museum? Believe me, it is not. At the heart of our lives and policies is this insistence on the unity of the glorious diversity of human experience. It may not come to the surface every day – nor does a heart – but it is there all the time, pumping life-blood through every aspect of the Museum's activities. For pedestrian purposes of organization

Sir Hans Sloane (1660–1753)

we have to divide our collections into departments and exhibit them accordingly. But each specialist knows perfectly well that practically every other department in the building can shed some light on his own special studies. The Rosetta Stone is only one literal example.

The practical side of this, the outward and visible sign of the essential unity, is the presence within the same building of what we call the 'antiquities departments' and what we call the 'library departments'. Here are these scores of thousands of objects, of all shapes, sizes and materials, from all dates and countries and continents, side by side in one building with seven million volumes of printed books and thousands of manuscripts, Western and Oriental, new and old, priceless and ephemeral. The sheer proximity of all these things is the practical manifestation of the theoretical unity. When you come here to write the definitive book on South Indian temple sculpture or Malayan war-canoe prows or medieval clocks or Assyrian lion-hunting you can see the relevant objects and then, a few yards down the passage, you can find all that has been written about them in English and a great deal in other languages as well. Clearly it is more convenient to be able to do this than to have to move from the museum part of your work at one end of Paris or New York to the library part of it at the other end. But the convenience is not the whole point. There is also the recognition of the interrelation between objects and other objects and between all of them and the books about them. I am often asked what is the British Museum's essential purpose and for whose benefit is it. To the second part of the question I shall return. My answer to the first part is that the British Museum is many things to many people, but for me its essential purpose is the documentation of human achievement. It does not matter whether the document is a manuscript or a printed book or a Greek statue or an Egyptian mummy-case or an Easter Island carving. Here is evidence of human achievement, of the work of man's mind and eye and hand. And it is that sort of documentation, the collecting of it, the conserving of it, the exhibiting of it, the publishing of it, that we are here to achieve. That, to me, is our essential purpose.

Let me return to the second half of the question which I asked a minute ago. For whose benefit, I am asked at least once a day, does the British Museum exist? Is it for the scholar, the specialist? Or is it for the general public, the ordinary man, woman and child? I refuse, with both honesty and logic, to accept this either/or way of putting it. The British Museum does not exist either for the scholar alone or for the general public alone. Our job is not either/or but both/and. There is a very wide range of people who legitimately have an interest in the place, a broad spectrum which contains almost exactly as many bands as the spectrum itself contains colours.

Firstly, there are our own resident experts, the Keepers of the various Depart/
ments. Each of them is a scholar of world/wide reputation, one of the recognized
authorities in his subject. It is his business, among all the other things he has to do,
to publish learned catalogues and critical works on the material in his particular
collection. The Keepers provide the fundamental basis of scholarship without
which the British Museum could not continue to be what it is. Secondly, there
are their expert colleagues from all over the world, devoted and exact scholars
who come from everywhere, Tokyo or Nebraska, Uppsala or Melbourne, to
work on the collections, with the collaboration of our Keepers. It is not always
recognized what an international workshop the so/called 'British' Museum is.
We are proud and glad to be the centre of so much peaceful international
activity. Thirdly, there are the individual scholars who are writing books, on
Chinese jade or the sociology of Indonesia or the private life of an eighteenth/
century poet. Not every one of them is a Marx or a Lenin or a George Bernard
Shaw. But they occupy the majority of the seats in the Reading Room on any
morning of the week. Then there are the individuals who are not writing great
tomes but are television producers, or feature/writers, or journalists, who want to
check on facts or fashions which are relevant to the particular programmes or
articles they are writing. And then there are the people, bless them, who work
in the area of Bloomsbury or Kingsway or Oxford Street, who come in for
twenty minutes a day on four days in the week in their lunch/hour just to look at
this object or that. They are in many ways the salt of our particular earth, and
over my dead body will the imposition of admission charges prevent them
from continuing their voluntary self/education. And then there are the coach/
loads of what might be called 'ordinary visitors'. Outside my window on any
day of the week I look at the back/end of buses, from Caterham or Darlington
or Brussels or Hanover, as well as those London/based ones which bring delega/
tions from Detroit or Dubrovnik. They may be 'sightseeing tours', or they may
be archaeological or artistic societies from the provinces visiting the British
Museum for a deliberate purpose. Or, again, there is the Great British Public,
each member with a greater or lesser degree of knowledge or previous experience.
Mum and Dad with one child in a push/chair and another in arms; or single/
tons who know what they want and do not wish to be either instructed or
disturbed; plain straightforward sightseers. And, finally, the thousands a week
of school/children, tumbling out of their coaches, charging round the galleries,
flattening their noses on the cases, greeting the mummies with contemporary
laughter (and some awe), and chattering like excited monkeys all the time.

Across that band – and I have tried to present it horizontally rather than
vertically – who shall presume to say for whom the British Museum exists? It
is not for any one of these categories to the exclusion of any of the others: it is for

all of them. With one proviso – which may seem pedantic and even a little pompous. None of the other categories could get what they want unless there were an absolutely firm foundation in the scholarly qualities of the Keepers, the resident academics. For on the quality of their work, in the acquisition of objects, in the proper display of the exhibits, in the books about them, in the free play of interpretation, the value of the place to everybody else must, in the long run, depend.

Again, I am asked about once a day what percentage of our possessions are not on view. The answer, if one is to be accurate, varies enormously from Department to Department. But the question itself seems to me to be based on a misunderstanding. It seems to be assumed that if we had enough room we should put on public exhibition all we possess. But this is not so. If we had all the room in the world we should not display to the public everything we have – for the simple reason that the public would not be interested in it if we did. Display is a comparatively new art, and we like to think that in our recently reorganized exhibitions of Greek and Roman, Assyrian and ethnographical objects we are using that art to some effect. The impact on the general public of a comparatively few objects from each Department, set out in the most attractive possible way, with appropriate lighting and adequate but discreet labelling, can be immense. Fifty Greek vases, set out shoulder to shoulder along a wall, make very little impact on anybody; and a thousand fragments of cuneiform tablet ranged mutely in a glass case would bore any ordinary person to tears. Display implies selection, and in this case selection of a few beautiful and striking examples of human achievement. All the rest of the collections are available to any scholar or antecedently interested person, in the secondary collections or in the stores. It is not always recognized that the number of objects we possess increases every week. Ours is not a static or finite collection. Every day something new comes in, by purchase or gift or bequest or exchange. But it does not at all follow that each of these newly acquired objects ought to be put on show at once – or, indeed, ever. It is as important to acquire a coin or a statue or a tribal object from Africa for the use of the scholar in that field as it is to acquire something which will have popular appeal for a few weeks. So suitable for public display is only one of the criteria which determine our acquisitions. Scholarship and its needs come in too, and quite independently.

That is a very quick sketch, from my personal point of view, of the institution which this book is about. I have to stress that this is my personal point of view because I fully recognize that each member of each of the bends of my spectrum will rightly and understandably have his or her own point of view too, and so will each of the twenty-five persons who constitute the Trustees of the British Museum.

This book introduces yet another dimension. For each of the contributions comes from what we have rather starkly regarded as 'an intelligent visitor'. The adjective is in one sense an insult, because, of course, all our visitors are equally intelligent – though perhaps some are more equally intelligent than others. And the noun too may be an insult, because all these contributors are much more than 'visitors', if that word suggests the casual dropper-in. Each of them has a deep personal interest in one particular part or aspect of our whole complex personality, though in their individual and collective modesty they would not set themselves up as experts. They are, if you care to put it so, interpreters; they have, each of them, their personal enthusiasms; and they know enough to be able to understand both the interpretations of the experts and the interests of those who know less.

We are greatly honoured that such a distinguished company of 'intelligent visitors' has been willing to take the time and trouble to interpret the British Museum to the world.

It is perhaps just worth adding to Sir John Betjeman's appreciation of Smirke's building that it will not be long, we hope, before a considerable addition is made to Smirke's own work. Mr Colin St John Wilson has designed an extension, to be built on the site's only remaining piece of building land, on the south-west corner immediately to the north of what is known as the 'Director's Office'. Here, beginning in 1972, will be added a four-storey building containing two galleries for temporary exhibitions (which at present can be mounted only in the King's Library), a centre for the Museum's developing educational services, and badly needed restaurants for the public and the staff.

Future plans, on the basis of a survey done by Mr Wilson, provide for adaptations to the Smirke building itself, which are intended to make more economical use of the space which Smirke provided without any violation of his principles.

And there is, of course, in prospect a great new building to the south side of Great Russell Street, to house the British Library of the future. But that is beyond our immediate concern.

Chapter One

Building the Museum

John Betjeman

To enjoy this mighty building to the full, is to appreciate its nature in terms of its inmates as well as its architecture. The staff probably look on other museums rather as the two older universities, Oxford and Cambridge, look on the red-brick and plate-glass universities. 'We were here first', and indeed they were. The British Museum was founded by Act of Parliament in 1753, a highly civilized time so far as arts and antiquities are concerned. It is not a Royal Palace taken over for the display of a republic's treasures as is so often the case in the rest of Europe. From the time of the Stuarts, private persons in Britain collected manuscripts, pictures, monastic records, State papers and books. Sir Robert Cotton in the sixteenth century and Sir Hans Sloane in the eighteenth, made famous collections which were of national importance. The space to house big collections was becoming difficult to find.

One of the Museum staff said to me 'In the Middle Ages we would have been a College. Because we were founded in the eighteenth century we are governed by trustees. Had we been founded in the nineteenth or this century, we would have been an Institution.' Trustees still govern the British Museum, but many incursions have been made on them by the civil service. Until 1963 the three principal trustees, *ex officio*, were the Archbishop of Canterbury, the Lord High Chancellor, and the Speaker of the House of Commons. There were also family trustees representing owners of the big collections. These trustees no longer hold office. The only *ex officio* trustee who survives is the one appointed by the monarch.

There is still an eighteenth-century air about the Keepers of Departments and other officials. The Keepers are dedicated specialists. If they write books at all, their book is a lifetime's work, probably a catalogue, but anyhow the last word on the subject. The members of the staff are very much characters, and they refer to the Museum as 'the House'. The lady cleaners are called 'the housemaids'. The uniformed officials are called 'warders'. Until well into the twentieth century they wore livery on important occasions such as Trustees meetings. The enormous entrance to the Museum where the porters sit, is still called the 'front hall', and its Superintendent at a monarch's visit wears the Windsor livery.

This hierarchical feeling of a country-house in the British Museum goes back

A night view of the British Museum's entrance and forecourt

to the days when it *was* a country House – Montagu House – in the flat fields of Bloomsbury, then outside London.

All country-house owners of education and taste assembled collections of pictures and antiquities, and the public was admitted on written application. Similar written application was necessary to see Montagu House, until 1810. Not until 1879 was the general public admitted on every weekday. Now it can come in on Sundays too, and there is electric light.

The Montagu House which housed the original British Museum, stood in front of the present building and where the cars are parked. It had been built for a Duke of Montagu whose descendant is the present Duke of Buccleuch. It was designed by Robert Hooke, a friend of Sir Christopher Wren. Colvin, in his *Dictionary of English Architects*, dates it 1675-9. Old water-colours of it show a red-brick house with stone dressings, rather like Kensington Palace. Inside there was a painted staircase, and at the top of this some stuffed giraffes. Stuffed animals were often part of a gentleman's collection in a country-house. That in the British Museum grew so unwieldy that the trustees caused a Natural History Museum to be built in South Kensington museumland.

What brought about the destruction of Montagu House, and the erection of the present building in 1823, was the presentation by George IV of his father's, George III's, enormous collection of books to the Museum. The Trustees commissioned Robert Smirke (1781-1867) to design the new building. Smirke himself, as a young man in 1803, had watched the marble frieze being removed

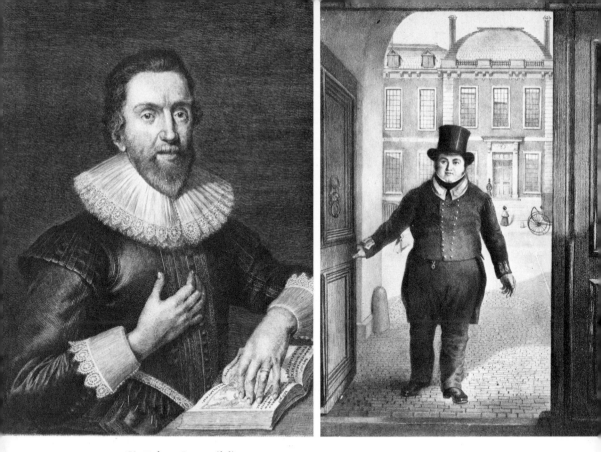

Sir Robert Cotton (*left*)

Entrance gate of the old building, Montagu House, at about 1840 showing a Museum servant wearing the Windsor Livery (*right*)

from the Parthenon with crowbars. This was sold by Lord Elgin, who had caused it to be removed, and bought by the nation in 1816, and it had to be housed in a temporary shed until Smirke had increased the size of the Museum.

Robert Smirke was an adventurous fellow and a man of few words. At the age of twenty he had gone with his elder brother to France to look at antiquities brought back to Paris by Napoleon. The brothers disguised themselves as Americans, and only just escaped capture. Smirke travelled to Italy and later to Greece, where he remained until 1805. He and his companion, William Walker, had to employ an army of brigands to fight off the other brigands, as at this time travelling in Greece was dangerous. Smirke managed things so well that he wrote, with the aid of his artist father, an illustrated manual called *A Review of the Battalion of Infantry*, which continued in use in the regular forces until 1840. When he returned to England in 1805, the Gothic style was becoming fashionable and Smirke designed Lowther Castle in this manner, and Eastnor Castle, which still survives in Herefordshire, he designed for Lord Somers in the Anglo-Norman style. He built many churches and public buildings in different parts of the country. He was well known for his rescue work, that is to say when an

Front quadrangle of the old building (Montagu House) in 1842; by John Wykeham Archer (*opposite above*)

Montagu House seen from the north-east; anonymous, *c.* 1800 (*opposite below*)

architect was in difficulties over the construction of an edifice, or if the foundations gave way, Smirke was called in. He was one of the first people to use concrete as a building material. He used iron plentifully in construction. He was honourable and precise about accounts, and is said to have originated 'that sound and useful custom of employing Surveyors to prepare proper bills of quantities for con⁄ tracts'. His character was calm and serene. He was knighted in 1832 in recog⁄ nition of his service to the Board of Works, which then controlled public buildings.

It was natural that in his design for the British Museum, Smirke should have employed his favourite Greek style. He has sometimes been dismissed as a dull architect, though so reliable and such a sound constructor. Several days of examining the architecture of the British Museum, have shown me that his calm assurance had with it decided, but honest and unostentatious originality. All details such as woodwork, doors, handles and ironwork, are most carefully scaled to the rooms or saloons in which they are placed. Colour is plain and sober but not sombre.

The most impressive thing about Smirke's architecture in the Museum is its scale. It is not until one comes up to the gigantic series of Ionic columns along the south façade of the Museum, that one realizes how huge they are. The jointing of the Portland stone in the pilasters and the walls behind, and in the columns themselves, is so meticulous and neat, that the building seems almost to have been carved from the solid rock. The same effect is produced in the magnificent and plain 'front hall'. The chief emphasis is on verticals and those are wide and strong. Oblongs and squares are the chief shapes in the front hall, and in its walls, and the columns, or coffers in the ceiling. The only curves are the flutings and Doric columns, and the delicate marble urns on the stairs. Smirke disliked horizontal features in his interiors and this makes itself apparent by the unfortun⁄ ate effect of horizontal woodwork recently introduced across the front door in the front hall, making nonsense of what was one of the grandest spaces in the whole building.

Smirke's work is seen at its best when viewed exactly from the middle. I know no walks in any public building anywhere to equal for serene simplicity, the procession one can make down the main stairs, through the Grenville Library and turning left to the great extent of the King's Library, all along the east front. The enormous length of the room is cleverly broken by a central square slightly wider than the rest of the library. Decoration in ceilings is of the plainest, but emphasizes the plan. Light falls from windows placed about two⁄thirds of the way up the walls, so that it is possible to read during daylight, without artificial light. If one compares Smirke's design for the British Museum with, let us say, Sir Aston Webb's Victoria and Albert Museum, South Kensington (1909),

Robert Smirke; a drawing by George Dance dated 30 July 1809

one notices the reticence of Smirke and the ebullience of Sir Aston Webb. Smirke's galleries are unobtrusive backgrounds to the exhibits; Sir Aston Webb's architecture intrudes into the exhibits and today has to be screened off with hardboard.

Smirke retired from practice in 1845, but lived until 1867. He was succeeded in office at the Museum by his faithful and competent younger brother Sydney (1799–1877). Sydney designed the iron railings which shut off the south front from the road, and which seem to me to be too near the great south façade. But Sydney was equally as bold an innovator as his brother Robert. When the great

Panizzi put new life into the Museum's Department of Printed Books, an enormous reading room was required. Robert had designed his Museum in the form of a square enclosing a rather gloomy stone courtyard. Panizzi made a rough sketch and showed this to Sydney Smirke, who designed the great dome, the second largest in the world after the Pantheon at Rome, over this courtyard. Thus he created the famous Reading Room. The spandrels between the dome and Robert's Museum he filled with cast-iron book stacks. Sydney Smirke's galleries, notably the Assyrian and those on the upper floors of his brother Robert's Museum, are reticent, practical, and unassertive. They are simply designed to display objects. Sydney Smirke, like his brother, was a public-spirited man. He founded the Architects' Benevolent Society in 1852, and was President of it until his death.

A third architect of distinction was employed by the Trustees in 1904. This was Sir John Burnet (1857–1938); he was a Glasgow architect who was trained at the Beaux-Arts in Paris. He designed the King Edward VII Galleries on the north side of Smirke's Museum. They were completed in 1914. The most distinguished feature of the Burnet design is neither its exterior nor the galleries themselves, but the marble staircase and ornamental gilded liftshaft at the north entrance. These are in a classic style, which would have amazed Smirke, but which are Edwardian at its lavish best. A bust of King Edward VII by Sir Thomas Brock is at the base. Marble stairs ascend to the galleries. A round marble well gives a view down to the basement. The huge columns and capitals shoot through floors. They are wholly original in scale and detail. Whereas Smirke is seen best from the middle wherever you look at his saloons, halls, stairs or façades, Burnet, because he was a Scottish Romantic, makes his Classical architecture best seen at an angle, and never all at once. Since Burnet's day no architecture of distinction has yet been added to the Museum.

Chapter Two

The Reading Room

J. E. Morpurgo

The Reading Room of the British Museum is the most wondrous, the greatest – if perhaps also among the least-beautiful cathedrals in the world, for here all gods are equal and equal too all devils, here is present all that is past, nation lives with nation and here, whosoever comes to seek will find – if only after a soul-testing delay appropriate to unhurried religiosity – some trace at least of all that man has achieved in the cause of beauty, vice, hate, love, entertainment, science – and downright silliness. Given a lifetime free from all other diversions and a know-ledgeable and pertinacious scholar might compile a list of a hundred books in the English language that are not here; a century scored, as it were, exclusively off no-balls. Equipped with the normal fortitude that goes with more humble scholar-ship – and with a reader's ticket – the ordinary explorer can sit at his desk, divert himself with speculations about the masterpieces that are being written all around him to be added eventually to the Museum's store, and in due course – in very due course – he will have brought to him almost any book or pamphlet in English; any book published in Britain since the passing of the Copyright Act of 1842, and most of what he might conceivably require in printed form in languages other than English.

Embraced, even smothered, by such awesome omniscience it is inevitable that he who attempts to describe is driven instead to illustrate by personal selec-tion. And, because the totality of all that is in books is too much for accounting and, even were it susceptible to definition, would still be beyond comprehen-sion, it is, I hope, at least forgivable if I slink back into the most convenient and most cowardly of all methods of expressing significance: autobiography. How-ever, if from this moment on, unashamedly I use the first person singular, it is not only because I know of no other way of reducing to reality the superhuman comprehensiveness of this collection, but also because hundreds of thousands of first persons singular have used the Library and each of them, in his own way, must have drawn from it some benefit, some experience, some pleasure or some frustration that sings rhyme to my own.

I have always been more easily moved by the creative electricity of the place than by its computer-like infallibility. It is the ghosts of the men who have used the Library that have meant most to me, not the vastness of the collection. Some

Sir Antonio Panizzi; an etching by J. Outrim after a painting by G. J. Watts, R.A.

have been here as pluralists, moonlighters, employees of the Museum and creators too. There was Henry Francis Cary, for example, who served the Library well in the second quarter of the nineteenth century, the period when, both in an architectural and in a bibliographical sense, it was setting to the forms that, to a large extent, persist to this day, but whose greater glory it was that he handed on to a century of English readers a poetically acceptable trans/ lation of Dante. There was Laurence Binyon, an interloper from the staff of the Print Room, whose unforgettable affirmation of remembrance of the war dead is inscribed in the walls of the main entrance hall of the Museum – and into the fabric of the consciences of millions. There was Angus Wilson, happily as yet no ghost, unless it be thought to be living death for a novelist to take on the spectral gown of a Professor of Literature.

Others came here to labour but not to be paid by the Trustees – not even by that temporally benevolent and eternally magniloquent Trustee, Lord Macaulay. They sit by me in the Reading Room, and pre-empt the reference-books that I must have from the open shelves. In accord with their earthly dispositions, or, sometimes I like to flatter myself, in response to what I have written about them even long after their deaths, some smile at me and some glower. Most often, as is the custom of the place that is acceptable alike to the bustling dead and to the egocentrically absorbed quick, they take no notice of me. Thackeray, at work on *Vanity Fair* or *Henry Esmond*, who had this same vision before me and owned to having said his 'grace at the table, and to have thanked Heaven for this my English birthright, freely to partake of these beautiful books'. His greater twin in the minds of readers and the compilers of school syllabuses, Charles Dickens. The unmistakable Bernard Shaw and his no less recognizable radio-rival, G. K. Chesterton. The poet W. B. Yeats staggers by:

> I spent my days at the British Museum, and must,
> I think, have been very delicate, for I remember
> putting off hour after hour consulting some
> necessary book because I shrank from
> lifting the heavy volumes of the catalogue.

and, after him, strange companions to the poets, playwrights and novelists, and yet by their very incongruity, symbolic of the catholicity of the place, Mazzini, and above all Lenin and Marx, unspeaking collaborators in preparing the way for the most seismic revolution of all time.

All these gigantic ghosts, and many of their lesser but still immortal spectral colleagues, have a diverting effect upon my easily diverted mind. Just as when I finger the catalogue on the way to filling out the form that is an essential pre-requisite to receiving some book that is imperative to whatever work I have in hand, I find my eye caught by some other – and to me entirely irrelevant but ineffably fascinating title – and call for that instead; so when Yeats, or Shaw, or Thackeray shatters the fragile vessel of my concentration my mind deserts my own puny labours – incidentally John Ruskin referred always to the Reading Room as his 'place of business' – and I set off an eager (or is it a servile?) search for their great achievements in print.

Presiding over all the glorious ghosts, all the eager living, over the great who have come here to establish and maintain their greatness, the rogues who have used this huge encyclopaedia of villainy to prepare their crimes, over the merely curious, and over the many poor devils who have come in just because they have nowhere else to go, and it is cold in the book-less world, there is one huge figure – huge both physically and in spirit – who has been dead for almost a

century but who in this place is no ghost at all. No ghost, because almost
every practice of the Reading Room in 1971 and its centrality to learning and
creativity was designed by him. He too was, by the judgement of his countrymen, a revolutionary, a conspirator, even an accessory to the murder of a 'Chief
Constable'. Strangest of all, and to any sturdy chauvinist, most humiliating,
this paramount genius of the British Museum Library – the institution which,
to my mind, has had no equal, except possibly the Royal Navy, as representative
symbol of Britain's greatness – was not himself British and even his name is
virtually unknown to the public, and to end but not to complete the series of
paradoxes, the book that I would choose from all the Museum's huge collection
to represent the man and the Library itself is one that I cannot read, that was
written before the Library as we now know it was thoroughly organized, a
book that he himself, in this one instance acting against all the accepted creeds
of respectable librarianship, later attempted to suppress; so successfully in fact
that there are, I believe, only two copies extant, one in his native Italy and the
other, most appropriately in the British Museum Library. The man is Antonio
Panizzi, a member of the staff of the Library from 1831, Keeper of Printed
Books – 'a papist . . . unknown in this country and unhonoured in his own'
promoted over the head of Henry Cary, 'a scholar and a poet of European reputation' who was also a Protestant clergyman and a Tory – Principal Librarian
from 1856 to 1866. The book, *Dei Processi*, is his own account of his early
Conrad-like, Graham Greene-like existence as what we have come to call a
Resistance worker, fighting from behind the mask of respectable law-officer and
an even more respectable position as a Civil Servant to the very power that he was
resisting, the brutal oppressions of his fellow officials in the tiny Duchy of
Modena. *Dei Processi* tells of the vicious trials which brought many of his friends
to the scaffold, and to him a death sentence *in absentia*, flight in the night, terror,
and years of enforced exile. As is not unusual in such stories the book was
written not so much to damn those who had persecuted him and the people he
sought to liberate from persecution, as to defend himself from accusations levelled
by his one-time fellow conspirators, he had been both coward and traitor to their
cause. The whole bloody, spy-thriller prologue seems unlikely and inconsistent
with Panizzi's later pacific career in the Museum. Modena, beastly behind its
beauty, un-Christian despite the supreme Romanesque loveliness of its cathedral,
seems an inconsequential prelude to the ponderous respectability of Victorian
Bloomsbury and the bloodless battles over the future of the British Museum
Library. Yet Panizzi remained a revolutionary for the rest of his long life and
the revolution that he wrought with idea, speech, wordy paper and bibliographical ingenuity was far more successful and far more enduring than his
youthful membership of secret societies or his cloak and dagger attempts to

Entrance hall of the old Building (Montagu House), 1845; by George Scharf (*above*)

The old Reading Room; by Thomas Hosmer Shepherd (*below*)

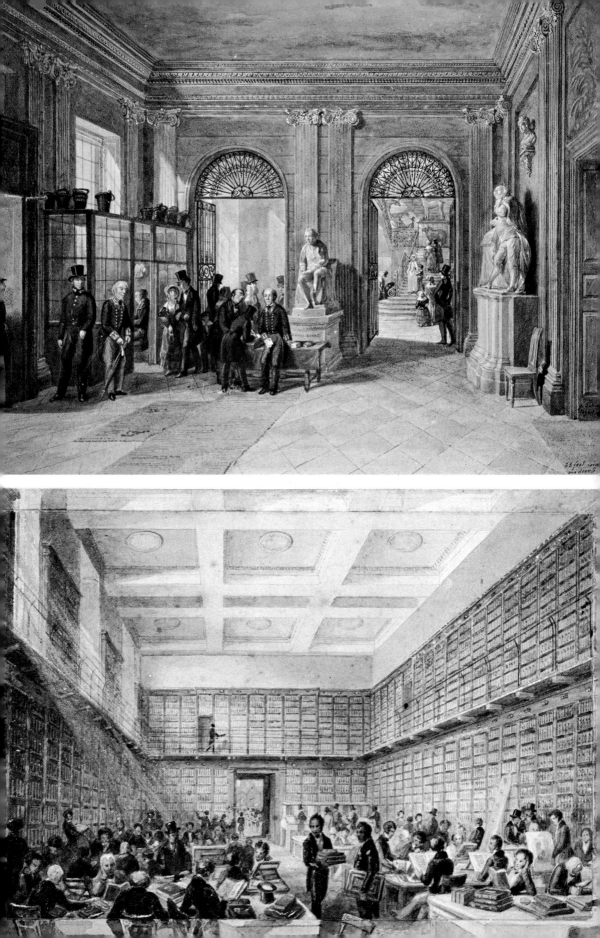

overturn a tyrannous princeling. He it was who brought to a successful conclusion the deposit clause in the Copyright Act and, if he failed to win for the Library the right to a second deposit copy that he coveted because he wished to use duplicate copies as the basis for a lending library, still, in due course, his vigorous efforts had some effect in creating the public library system which we now enjoy. Panizzi did argue his way to receiving from Government adequate funds for buying books – old books and foreign books – not covered by the deposit arrangements. He suggested the designs of the Reading Room and the Iron Library. He invented the method of labelling books, and devised the first truly systematic catalogue – though, alas, even after several revisions, it seems today to be an antisystem that is dedicated to the task of delaying the reader, even of frustrating him beyond endurance. It is said that it was Panizzi who first introduced a staff canteen into a public institution!

It was when I was working on Charles Lamb and James Henry Leigh Hunt that I first used the Library. Both were schoolfellows of mine, though a century and a half my seniors. Lamb, though somewhat out of popularity is still, I suspect, a familiar figure to all who read. Leigh Hunt, in his day the greatest and most courageous of editors, the man who first recognized the genius of Shelley and Keats, who encouraged Byron – and went to prison for his attacks on the Prince Regent – is now almost forgotten and if he is remembered at all is known only for two of the worst poems in the anthologies, 'Jenny kissed me' and 'Abou ben Adhem'. Both disliked the villain of this chapter in my story, Thomas Carlyle. Both were attacked by him. And Carlyle, that sour Scot, turned his considerable ability for abuse also upon Panizzi and upon Panizzi's Library. Lamb, though he did not know Panizzi and did not live to see even the first fruits of Panizzi's great labours, loved the old Montagu House Library, recognized that it could be developed and almost certainly would have supported enlargement and improvement. But the triangular tournament, though it can only be deduced from the characters of the three men and from what they wrote, is not as simple as it first appears. Lamb was a close friend of Cary and, such was his capacity for loyalty, undoubtedly would have sided with him against Panizzi in the struggle for appointment as Keeper. And, what is worse for me when I attempt to act as referee by transposing ancient comment into modern observation I am reluctantly forced to give the verdict to Carlyle against both Lamb and Panizzi. 'You have scarce to ask for a volume before it is laid before you,' said Lamb. Not so Carlyle. For him the Reading Room was far too crowded and lacked facilities for private and continuous study (a shortage which to this day, and however democratic its inspiration, sets the Museum lower on the scale of scholarly utility than many of the other great libraries of the world). It also lacked a sensible catalogue. It does still.

Back to Charles Lamb, to my private pleasure in the Library – and to one of those unimportant discoveries that are all-important to me (as I hope to any sensible time-waster, whatever direction his own particular enthusiasm for time-wasting may take). Because I had been at school in the spaciousness of Christ's Hospital in Sussex I felt that I must attempt to rid myself of the sense that Lamb's school-days, and Leigh Hunt's, had been passed in similar surroundings. Intellectually, I knew that it was not so, that the pre-1902 school in Newgate Street, London was at once more beautiful and far more like a slum. I had seen single prints from Ackermann's *Great Schools of England* but never the whole book, not even the whole Christ's Hospital set. I sent for the volume – and I was seeing the school that Lamb and Leigh Hunt had seen. I was seeing it, too, as another had known it, Charles Lamb's closest friend but in the canons of English literature far greater even than Elia: Samuel Taylor Coleridge. It was now Coleridge that I sought to discover. Having passed his portrait several times a day during the seven years of adolescence, his face I knew as well as my own in the mirror. I was not, for the moment, concerned with the wonders of *The Ancient Mariner*, the superlative ramblings of *Biographia Literaria*, not even with the major events in Coleridge's troubled life. I was chasing trivia, the little things that, so often far more than the great, transform a man's life, and that, in the case of Coleridge, might help to explain that reiterated snapping-off of endeavour just short of superlative achievement. I thought of his vast scholarship and remembered that his father, who had thought no vastness except the size of his family (thirteen – of whom Samuel was the youngest), had also been a considerable Classical scholar; remembered too that the Reverend John Coleridge had also written a book. In the North Library, the left luggage room for the Museum's rarer bibliographical items, I wrote out my slip for John Coleridge's revised Latin Grammar. It came to me, and though I never read one word of print, I was for the first and perhaps for the only time in my life in direct contact with the great Romantic by ways of a signature in browning ink on the fly-leaf of a book. For a moment I sat awed by the immediacy of the past, and then, awakened to my responsibilities as a citizen but still trembling with excitement, I took the book to the guardian librarian. Should such a rarity as this be available to any who asked? Should it be handled? Should it not be kept under glass? He listened with some patience to my incoherent expostulation, and then (I hope he will forgive me, but I like to think that he was Angus Wilson) dismissed me forever. 'Oh, we have thousands like that.'

Any bookman or for that matter any book-lover who frequents the Museum, although he must accept without question that the Library is not the exclusive property of those who practise the book-arts, and although his everyday custom will have demonstrated to him that the Library's prime function is compre hensiveness and not the preservation of beauty or rarity, will none the less from time to time worship at the shrines of the book-crafts. The forty-two-line Gutenberg Latin Bible, the first substantial book printed from movable type, took its makers more than a year to prepare and, even after 520 years of ever-increasing competition, it remains one of the finest examples of typographical skill. There are but forty-eight copies in existence. Thirty-six printed on paper and twelve on vellum. The Library owns one of each. They are, in the most severe sense, museum pieces; I look at them with awe; I dare not touch; they do not belong to me. But the pocket editions produced in Venice by Aldus Manutius just as the fifteenth century became the sixteenth: these are mine; these are the true predecessors to the ten humble-seeming books that appeared on 30 July 1935.

Those first Penguins, published at sixpence each, seem in retrospect an unlikely prelude to a revolution in education, reading-habits and taste. A collection of now-forgotten or but dimly remembered titles with only one indisputable classic, there was among them no science, no scholarship, none of that instant political or social comment that was later to make Penguins famous. And the appearance of the books was as unsensational as the selection of titles. A simple colour code – orange and white for the novels, green and white for the detective stories, blue and white for the biographies – was the only break with parsimony and austerity. Yet in a very real sense these ten books were the obverse to the Museum Library, for they began a movement which has reached almost every country in the world and which has made it possible for every man to build in his own sitting-room his own polymathic library. Penguins were to play a considerable part in my professional career but for me, as for millions the world over, that Friday before the August Bank Holiday of 1935, is the day of the miracle that turned me from book-reader to book-collector.

However, if I have been fortunate in that I have been allowed to make a career – several careers – out of my passions and pastimes, and all of them have brought me frequently to the Museum – even at one time to membership of one of its highly technical ancillary committees – I have been doubly fortunate in that my principal scholarly interest ties me and the Library to my second home, North America. For, as anyone can hear who chooses to listen to the voices on the steps outside, the Museum and especially the Library is international and, particularly, almost as much an American as a British institution.

I, and thousands before me, have sought in vain for some answer to the mystery of what happened to the second British colony in America, the City of Raleigh in Virginia, and to the first English child born in America. Virginia Dare's birthdate we know, the 18th of August 1587, but for the rest history is unaware of her existence and the existence of most of the adults who were of that

The modern Reading Room

'Discomfortable Company' for only another eight days passed before they disappear into the mists of speculation and tragedy.

But Virginia Dare's grandfather left for England on the ninth day of her life to seek reinforcements and supplies for the tiny colony, and through his eyes and his pen what they saw – and perhaps saw in the last horrific moments before they were massacred – is revealed in the uneventful calm of Bloomsbury.

Some historians argue that the massacre – if massacre it was that destroyed the second colony – did not take place for almost another twenty years, until just before the arrival of the group of English men and women who created the first permanent settlement, and that their death was ordered by Powhatan, the great Indian King and father of Pocahontas. Any mention of Pocahontas sets most minds to thinking of the romantic story of the man who was saved from death, Captain John Smith. The sceptic in me knows that John Smith was a great romancer, much given to exaggerating his own importance and to embroidering his own escapades. But the addict in me is aroused by Pocahontas. She married John Rolfe, and Rolfe has his place in history not so much for this essay

in miscegenation as because he was the first to cure tobacco so as to make it pala-
table to European tastes. I grope for a cigarette – and the implacable rule of the
Museum drives me out of the Library, if it is winter to shiver for my sins under
the great portico, if it is summer to enlarge upon those sins by lascivious study of
the latter-day successors to Pocahontas, the pretty girls who have followed her
back from America to England. Their dress is scantier than the ridiculous
Jacobean garments in which Rolfe encased his wife. I hope that they will not
find, like her, that even an English summer is treacherous, and so come to their
death of cold at Gravesend. I hope that they will not even go to Gravesend.

> When I was a young man I used to read books
> In a place called the British Museum.
> There were plenty of women who gave me strange looks
> But sometimes I just didn't see'em.
>
> Now I am ninety and weary of books.
> Of knowledge (I think) I have plenty.
> Now; I'm beginning to notice the girls –
> They are most of them round about twenty.
>
> If I polish my glasses I see them quite well,
> And some are exceedingly pretty,
> It occurs to me that I have wasted my life,
> And there goes the bell. What a pity!

Thus, Sydney Carter, to my knowledge the only poet to have written and published two poems about the Museum, in the more irreverent of the two. He it was
who was my regular whispering companion in the Reading Room, twenty-
odd years ago when I set off on the quest for an answer to another Anglo-
American mystery which had its origins at the end of the same century that
saw the 'Nonpareil of Virginia' dead at Gravesend, and in a place that is less
than ten miles from the place where Pocahontas's husband founded the fortunes
of Virginia against *The Counterblaste* of his royal master.

There, at the College of William and Mary, the oldest academic building in
continuous use in North America is confidently described to the millions of
tourists who gawp their way through Restored Williamsburg as the Wren
Building, the only building outside Britain designed by the architect of St
Paul's Cathedral. The ascription is based on one remark made by a near-
contemporary who had reason to know, but though I (and hundreds of others)
have scurried through everything that is in this Library (and a dozen more) that
should, could, or conceivably might, affirm as historical the fable that I would
like to believe, after twenty years my faith is failing. True, the Wren Building

has some family resemblance to the Chelsea Hospital; the Hospital is undeniably Wren's and the likeness was commented upon by the very man who started the rumour. But, as I have found to my delight but to the increase of mystification – and of the physical labours of so many of the Library's staff – so does every other public building designed about 1700 look as if it were by Wren.

It is no great leap from one of the founders of the Royal Society to a living Fellow, a man who regards Wren's dome for St Paul's as a source for the inspiration that has led him to devise, for our own century and the next, engineer-ing marvels that are also, like Wren's, aesthetically magnificent. And, if it may seem the foolhardiness of a pygmy attempting to jump the Giant's Causeway that I, who came here first to study Coleridge and Lamb, stayed on to consider ancient explorers and then bustled after Wren, have in the last few years spent much time in the Library, seeking material for a life of Sir Barnes Wallis, there is a logic behind the boldness which Sir Barnes would be the first to grasp.

The personal prejudices of Antonio Panizzi, which favoured always the arts against the sciences, for a long time held back his Library from achieving comprehensiveness and even today, because post-Panizzi legislation has set up in other places libraries specifically for the sciences, there are collections that are of more immediate utility to the scientist himself. Happily, the White Paper published in January of 1971 proposes the return to Bloomsbury of all the nation's central library resources, but even now before the reunion takes place, the deposit clause in the Copyright Act, the geographical centrality of the Museum and the very fact that here all science and art is under one roof – may they perish who would fragment the collection – makes this still the best-equipped storehouse for the student who seeks knowledge of the sciences and of their relation to politics, economics and the whole social structure of this as of other nations. I was not visiting the Library to prepare myself to design an air-ship or test a bouncing bomb. I was not called upon to utilize the theory of variable geometry; not even to discover what that theory is; for all these things and for much more I had the freedom of Sir Barnes's papers and the assistance of his superb didactic skill. What I needed, and to a considerable extent dis-covered within the Library, was some understanding of the reasons that lay behind a long history of unique originality frustrated, of ingenuity thwarted, of opportunity, offered to Britain by an Englishman, forever being seized and exploited by other nations. I cannot suggest that even for this or for any major historical or biographical project, the printed book can ever be the major source. Again, the papers of Sir Barnes, recollections and documents provided by others, the Public Records Office – and, incidentally, the Museum's newspaper collection which is not housed in Bloomsbury – were to me in many ways more important than all the books in the Library. But, as an example within an

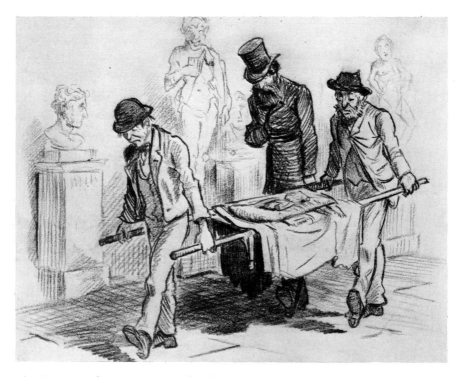

The Ceremony of removing a piece of sculpture in the Museum;
by Randolph Caldecott (1846–86)

example, when I came to consider the hideous story that ended with Wallis's magnificent *R 100* in a breaker's yard and with its bumbling rival, the *R 101*, tragically destroyed on a French hillside, the Library was beyond value. With memoirs, biographies and histories of those years that ended in 1930, I could reconstruct, I hope with some perspicacity, the sad record of unnecessary opposition, misplaced ambition, political chicanery, and downright incompetence which brought some men to hideous death at Beauvais, and wrote for Wallis a premature finish to what I have come to regard as even so his greatest achievement, greater than the indestructible Wellington, Swallow or the bouncing bombs designed for him by Sir Michael Redgrave.

Carlyle claimed that 'there are several persons in a state of imbecility who come to read in the British Museum'. But, if it be madness to believe what is denied by experience and reason, then the authors who come here to write, are even closer to lunacy than the rest, for, as most authors will admit, all believe and, until they read the reviews all must hope, that it is the latest of their books which is the most important. I am no exception; the freak addition to my bibliography, the life of Wallis, is for this moment my cloak of glory.

But any author who has in him a grain of honesty will confess that he aspires to immortality; given two grains and then he must accept that the very statistics of this Library are against him: 7 million volumes in the collection, and, from Britain alone, almost 30,000 new titles added each year. His only certainty of a life to all time for his books is as a tiny digit in those horrific statistics; his only sure memorial is here in the catalogue of the British Museum Library.

Still, nightmarish in his day-dreams, there is the book that he did not write, the one indubitable masterpiece that was never finished. I have mine: a life of John André. A plaque on a house in Bath, a lonely memorial not far from Sing Sing and West Point, an American folk-ballad in his honour, a casual mention in an essay by Lamb, a place among the regimental heroes of British regiments that no longer exist to honour their heroes, a hideous monument among the litter of hideous monuments that deface Westminster Abbey, and a series of foot-notes by authorities on military law are all that remain to the memory of the soldier-poet-actor-secret agent-painter-engineer who died in the fading moments of the War of Independence at the end of an American rope, and was mourned as much by those who condemned him as by his own countrymen. When I began to work on his life in the British Museum Library I saw André as the epitome of eighteenth-century dilettantism, saw him too as the strangely off-centre focus for the struggle of conscience that separated the two great English-speaking nations. Certainly all the major – and many of the minor but still-remembered characters of the American Revolutionary period and from both sides of the Atlantic, were intimately involved with André: Washington, Lafayette, Alexander Hamilton, Arnold, Howe, Erasmus Darwin, Dr Johnson, Lord North. The story had everything – that I knew – romance, espionage, treachery, courage, wit and, at the last, tragedy. But if I knew it, so it seemed did every other author working in the British Museum and the Library of Congress. Each time I settled to research a publisher somewhere announced a life of André. I hesitated. Either the rival book did not appear at all or when it appeared it was rich only with inaccuracies. There were two films – even further from history than the books. My own ambitious project degenerated into a radio play.

Perhaps these are the true ghosts of the Library: the books that have never been written.

I watch the eager readers, the busy scribblers at the desks in the Library, and I I am at once both comforted and pitying. The statistics are on my side after all, for there must be spectres more restless even than the unfinished books: the books that have been written but never published and never read.

Chapter Three

Prints and Drawings

Michael Ayrton

Nearly everything I do, or have ever done, stems from the practice of drawing. It is one of the principal ways by which I order my thoughts, and whether I am painting, or making sculpture, or even writing, all my work is some sort of extension from drawing. Drawing is a method of thinking and I learned to think that way in the British Museum Print Room.

Like all sweeping statements, that is only partially true. I learned to think as best I could, just as I learned to draw, in all sorts of places. I learned to draw in the Louvre in Paris, and in the Uffizi in Florence, and in the Albertina in Vienna and, like many another aspiring draughtsman, I learned from looking very hard at the world about me and drawing from nature. I truly believe, however, that I learned my craft from my predecessors as much, if not more, than from 'life'. It was they who taught me to see, for the simple reason that they did it so much better than I ever shall.

I arrived in the Print Room, with my father, when I was twelve years old, and sat down, in great awe, at a table in the Department. There I was given a box of mounted drawings by Albrecht Dürer to examine. I turned them over slowly, under the eagle eye of the great A. E. Popham, one of the foremost scholars in the field of Master Drawings and later Keeper of the Department. I remember the occasion with piercing clarity. It was a dark November day in 1933. Taking hold of the drawings made me so nervous that my hand shook.

In the school holidays thereafter, I went to the Museum almost every day and was granted a ticket to the Print Room – a special concession of which I was inordinately proud. It was to me like being taken on to the footplate of the *Flying Scotsman*. And from the Print Room I used to go to a print-shop near by where with infinite patience, I was advised by the proprietor as to how to spend my pocket-money. It was there that I bought Dürer's woodcut, *St George* (1), for a saved-up ten shillings and, since it was an early impression on Bull's Head paper, I wish I had it now. It was a print, but an original print from the original wood-block. It was a real Dürer, not a mechanical reproduction, and this was as important to me as a genuine Cape Triangle would have been to a schoolboy stamp-collector. Paradoxical as it may seem, the print was to me first and fore-most a drawing made in a form I could afford, and this, of course, is one of the

1. Dürer, *St George*; Woodcut, *c.* 1505

2. Michelangelo, *Reclining Male Nude* (Study for the Sistine Chapel *Creation of Adam*);
Red chalk, *c.* 1511

primary reasons why prints were and are made. They circulate images in the way
that letterpress printing circulates writing. It was not the expertise of prints –
the stamp-collecting angle, with the special knowledge of states and condition
and watermarks of the paper, which makes the true collector so happy and so
crazy – it was *the image* that concerned me. It still does. I am not a collector,
except haphazardly. I am an image-maker, by vocation, by profession and by
instinct. I also have a keen awareness of my superiors, those masters who taught
me what mastery I have, in the Print Room at the British Museum and everywhere else where their work is to be found.

The Print Room or, to give it its full title, the Department of Prints and Drawings, was created in 1808. It houses so many thousands of examples of drawings
and water-colours and of prints in the form of engravings, etchings, woodcuts
and lithographs that no one really knows even now just how many items it
contains. But certainly it is the world's greatest collection.

What, then, is this need to draw and why have so many, during so many centuries, sought with such agony to master the skill of making significant graphic marks on flat surfaces? It is very old, this need. It is certainly 30,000 years old. It is concerned with 'beauty', but not as much as many people think. It is con- cerned with recording visual phenomena, but not as consistently as people assume. It is part of 'self-expression' – that popular excuse for art – but less with self-expression than with the visual examination of forms *outside the self*. It is everything from the absent-minded doodle to the masterpiece of the concentrated mind and the matchless hand. Aristotle said that 'art completes what nature cannot finish', and as usual with Aristotle, what he said makes sense. Nature is unmanageable. It is too rich, too seemingly disordered, too protean, for man to cope with, unless he can create order in it. To make images, by drawing, by sculpture, by painting, by print-making, or by any other method, is only very peripherally a matter of aesthetics. It is an act of power. It is to master and to order appearances. It is as much to act out the most ancient of combats, the combat with forces beyond man's control, to contest with such opposing forces in nature as weather, growth, the coming of winter and all the natural menaces which threaten man's well-being, as it is to celebrate the joy of that well-being. It is not sketching to please one's mum. It is struggling to hold, to grip the appearance of reality and to subdue it by means of handmade marks which magically control the measure of man's power over his environment. It is also to give thanks for the benevolent aspects of that environment.

All this is pretty sententious stuff, but it is truer than the notion that peculiar individuals spend, and have spent, their lives in this onerous and endless specialized activity in order to make fame, or fortune, or soothe and placate connoisseurs. Drawing, like any other art, is an invention. It is the result of using the imagination to alter what things look like in order to make them look more intensely 'like' what they are than they appear to the casual eye.

Faced with heaven knows how many thousands of images and how many hundreds of ways of making them, with an infinite number of subjects covering every known sight and spectacle: from rural landscapes to classical allegories, from portraits of notables to portrayals of marvels, from pedestrian topography to paranoid fantasies, from architectural extravagances to storm-tossed seascapes, from sober townscapes to visions of God, and from minute studies of grass and flowers to grand designs for royal processions – I must make some sort of choice in all this plethora of what men have seen and thought it necessary to represent on paper. Regretfully, I have decided to pass by the tremendous collection of Turner's water-colours which he left to the nation, the wonderful group of Watteau's chalk-drawings, and the landscape-drawings of Claude Lorrain. Instead I shall discuss only a handful of drawings and almost all of them are nudes. I choose nudes because I myself belong to the tradition which sets the

3. Antonio Pollaiuolo, *A Prisoner led before a Judge*; Pen and brown ink, *c.* 1460

undraped human form – man in God's image – at the very centre of the act of drawing.

The Greeks 'invented' the nude. They did so because of the nature of the Greek mind, making of it an abstraction which was to them more real, more timeless and more divine than nakedness. This they did by relating mathematics to the proportions of the human figure, which they believed (and who will argue?) to be the most 'true' and perfect of divine inventions. Man, being man, inevitably considers the most important and the most satisfactory of all relationships of form to be the human body. It was this ideal, the Classical ideal of the human body as a relationship of units, 'perfectly' and harmoniously reconciled to one another, to which the Greeks gave pre-eminence. They made their gods conform to it. Of course, naked figures were drawn, painted and carved before the Greek 'invention', but such was the power of the Greek imagination and such was the weight of their power as image-makers, that they made the naked human figure into the cardinal measure of excellence by which all other things might be seen and judged, including architecture.

There are all sorts of other kinds of drawing. There are cultures, like those of China and the Muslim world, which are quite unconcerned with, or religiously opposed to, any concern with the nude. There have also been long periods in

Europe – one of some 1300 years – when the nude was more or less outlawed from the arts. It crept in when absolutely necessary, as in the case of Adam and Eve, but it was generally a cypher. Nevertheless, so powerful was the Greek idea about the human body that during the thirteenth century it gradually re-emerged, and suddenly, early in the fifteenth century in Italy, it returned in splendour. From that day forward, the nude re-established itself as the core and heartbeat of the Western European tradition of drawing.

Drawings we have, of one sort and another, from Palaeolithic times scratched in caves, carved on bones and incised on pottery. But for the period before the fourteenth century drawings in the special sense, by which we mean the marks on paper housed in the British Museum Department of Prints and Drawings, do not exist, except as papyrus and manuscript illumination, which are rather different and special fields. And we have precious few drawings produced as early as the fourteenth century. Thus in Renaissance Italy there was a twin development. The nude in the Greek sense was restored and, one way and another, drawing as mostly we tend to think of it today, was born. That tradition, whether anyone likes it or not, is ours. Drawing as a discipline and as a joy, rests firmly and predominantly on the nude.

The nude is a very odd thing. It has, of course, I am happy to say, close

4. Dürer, *Apollo and Diana*; Pen and brown ink, *c.* 1501–3 (*left*)

5. Dürer, *The Fall of Adam* (Adam and Eve); Engraving, 1504 (*right*)

association with sex. It has also a great deal to do with the fact that as individuals we all inhabit, each to his own, a nude. In my own case, it is a wearisome and, to me, an unattractive sack of tripes with dreary demands and various chronic aches and pains, but its structure is me. It is timeless since, although fashion shapes the desirable body as readily as it does the dress we wear, there is yet a consistency in its disposition of the parts, the units of which it is combined, which varies more from the condition and age of the individual's anatomy than from any fundamental change in their form. In this respect it is art that completes and reorganizes nature's inadequacy.

The Greeks admired the athlete, much as we do, but a very great deal more. For them, as the poet Spenser put it for the Elizabethans, 'soul is forme and doth the bodie make'. And *form* in its relation to the spirit, no less than to the physique, is what the art of drawing is about.

The greatest of all masters of the nude is Michelangelo. He was concerned with practically nothing else. There is, in all his work, and he lived to be eighty-nine, virtually no landscape, no still-life, none of the myriad natural phenomena which so obsessed his older and equally great contemporary Leonardo da Vinci. He could and did contain his genius in the structure of the

6. Michelangelo, *Crucifixion*; Black chalk, *c.* 1560

human frame, and when he clothed or draped his figures, it is the human body, existing within or behind the clothing, which determines and shapes the form. For him and for him alone among the giants, the human frame itself was all that was needed.

He began, because he was from the outset a sculptor and concerned with the weight of forms, by drawing copies of the paintings of his great predecessors Giotto and Masaccio who, when the Renaissance itself was in the womb, brought *weight* back into painting, weight heavily and magisterially draped. Then for a long lifetime he described the human body, first with abrupt strokes of the pen and then more fluidly with chalk. When in doubt he drew across and into the form, aiming to establish its boundaries and to depict the illusion of its weight, moving his eye and hand over and under the taut or slack muscles, each dependent in its tension or relaxation upon the complex interrelated forms which, as bones and sinews, make it possible for the human body to act. All the underlying structure of a great mountain landscape could be read into the torso and legs of one of his drawings (2); the rock hardness of the bones which lie just below the skin and jut out at the knees, the fallow softness of the great relaxed muscle suspended like a rolling hillside below the thigh. Disdaining error, he would restate a contour, in this instance the line which marks the turning-point of the top of the leg, where the form moves out of sight, correcting three times. This he does because, in the act of drawing, he is discovering exactly where that contour should be. He is exploring. He is finding out for himself, *and for himself alone*, the boundaries and shapes of flesh animated by sinews, strung on a frame of bone. Given seventy-five years of continual drawing, he would know, as no one else has ever known, how, on the flat surface of a small piece of paper, the components of that envelope of flesh we all inhabit, may definitively be set down. Or you might imagine he would. But it was not so. In old age and with undiminished power (he was carving marble three days before he died) he came to doubt these exact dispositions of form. His latest and most mysterious drawings (6) emerge from the paper like a mist, a cloud of tentative strokes of the chalk, no longer concerned to map the limits of the limbs, the contours, but drawn from inside them, so that the forms seem at once dense and breathing. Such drawings are miraculously remote from the tight and precise delineations of the youthful pen. They are indeterminate concretions of doubt, built from a deeply humble uncertainty as to where forms begin and where they end, because they breathe and endlessly move, because there is no real stillness in nature and because only God knows how the flesh holds in the spirit. This indeed exemplifies that 'soul is forme and doth the bodie make'.

The kind of drawing which was developed in fifteenth- and sixteenth-century Florence was called *disegno*. It was a clear, tough and very specific approach to

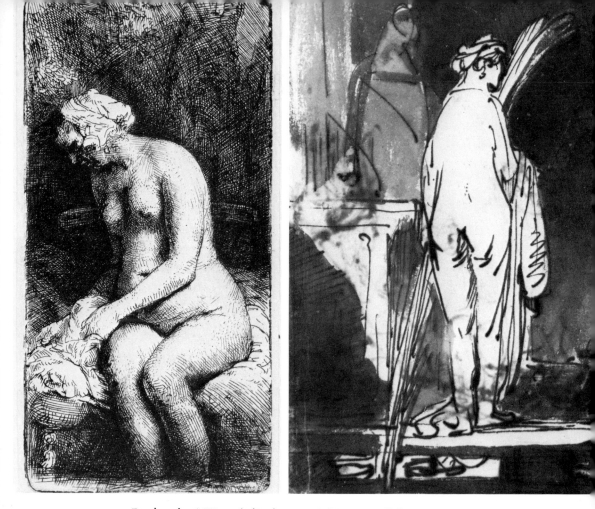

7. Rembrandt, *A Woman bathing her Feet*; Etching, 1658 (*left*)
8. Rembrandt, *Study for the Etching: The Artist drawing from a Model* (detail);
Pen and brown ink, *c.* 1639 (*right*)

form, and the nude, energetically but carefully studied, took its form from
the Greek and Roman antiquities being enthusiastically excavated in Italy at that
time. Roman marbles gave the mandate for Renaissance artists to seek to
match Antique ideals unearthed in the recovered fragments of a lost Golden
Age. And even now this tradition continues.

The long hibernation of the concept of the nude ended in the fifteenth
century, but it took some time for the human body unswathed with draperies
to extend from the Mediterranean area, where indeed it had both been born and
reborn, and move north. One man, more than any other, took it there. Albrecht
Dürer, a German, who trained as an engraver, and whose genius in that field
and as a draughtsman outranks his ability as a painter, learned to master the
Classical nude. It took him half a lifetime of concentration to do it, to compre-
hend the undraped human body to the degree of harmonious certainty he felt
it needed. He began in the Gothic tradition of the North which had long dis-

pensed with those geometrical canons of proportion by which the Greeks set such store and which the Italians had first dimly and then triumphantly remembered. He imposed a form of geometry on his nudes and wrote a book on human proportions seeking that just relationship, that 'rightness' which his Florentine predecessors had called *certezze*: the 'certainties'. Rembrandt owned a copy of Dürer's book on human proportions.

Dürer studied Italian engravings of the nude by Antonio Pollaiuolo (3) and by Andrea Mantegna, who were among the first great draughtsmen of the Renaissance nude and the pioneer engravers in Italy. He made careful copies of their work and then adapted it. At this point the engraved copper plate and the wood-block, the print, really came into its own.

Without prints the vital information could not travel from place to place unless the artist himself travelled with his work, as Dürer did, to Venice in 1507. Prints could readily be packaged and sent. They were also cheap. By those means the inventions, the developments in composition, the refinements of proportion could be transmitted from artist to artist across the Continent and no one, not even the greatest, least of all Rembrandt or Rubens, disdained to make use of them. Originality was not a fetish in those days and no false shame was attached to copying. The fame of Dürer himself travelled with his prints. Engravings and woodcuts in hundreds left his shop to circulate through Europe, and the fact that they still do enabled me to buy one or two when I was at school.

From my schoolboy addiction to Dürer, I turned elsewhere. I rejected, in my adolescence, so earnest, noble and precise an art and turned, as, I suppose, was natural enough, to what seemed to me more 'natural'. I turned to Rembrandt, whose genius is so deep that he could make the most intricate, calculated and intellectually considered images look as if they were simply produced by looking, not at art, but at nature. Rembrandt's nudes look like naked people (7, 8, and 9); the huge artifice is buried. They look 'true' in what seems a most straightforward, but is in fact a very complicated, way, but they owed as much to his close study of arts which had come out of Italy and from as far off as India, as to his unsurpassed mastery of natural forms described by strong light contrasted with deep shadow. This fascinated me but it was, I thought, simply a matter of his looking hard at people and things in that sort of light and dark context. I was right and wrong.

I had not understood then the implications of the point I am making now about how artists have, in every age, unblushingly taken what they needed from their predecessors. Nor did I know, despite the huge quantity and seemingly wide variety of images to have been built up since the Greeks, how constant the mainstream of forms had been.

Like any aspiring young artist, I wanted to be original, and uniquely myself. I need not have been so shy about my borrowings. Dürer was not alone in copying Mantegna. Rembrandt, too, did so and the drawing, here illustrated, of the *Calumny of Apelles* (10) was once owned by Rembrandt, for it was a leaf in 'the precious book of Mantegna' which figured as Item 200 in the inventory of Rembrandt's property made in 1656. If, as seems likely, he copied (11) this drawing in 1655, he was no aspiring art student but a master aged fortynine and so far original and uniquely himself that he had no cause to take shame in seeking what he needed from the history of the art he so greatly enriched. He used what he required from his carefully assembled collection of prints and drawings by Mantegna, his prints after Titian and Raphael, but he took as much and more from his fellow human beings. That was the equation, and the nude is central to it. The human body is both to be drawn and to be embraced, and the drawing is in itself an embrace.

By then I was, I think naturally, much concerned with real human bodies. I was fifteen or sixteen at the time. Those bodies, although highly attractive, were very often far from ideal and whatever other relations I had with them, I was drawing them every day, year in year out, from 'nature' in art schools. It took me years to discover that, contrary to precept, nature is simply too clever, too complex and too secretive to give herself away to art students. You have to enlist the powers of the great masters in order to master any part of nature. The whole history of art demonstrates this. You have to imitate art and this you do naturally, as you develop, but not always very wisely. Nor do you inevitably know, or understand, what you are borrowing. As I grew up I was, like any student, inundated with visual information. I was lucky; I travelled about Europe. Influences, styles, contemporary manifestation, came rushing in. Art books began to proliferate; I gulped away at it all. It was confusion of the most intoxicating kind, as I remember, and much of it was as halfbaked as I was.

At this point when, even if I did not quite know it, I needed it most, the British Museum closed down for six years and the museums of Europe were all in enemy hands. There was, as people relentlessly pointed out, a war on.

Before the nineteenth century the number of great drawings available for study must have been fairly limited for any but the most fortunate of practising artists. If he had access to private cabinets of drawings, he was indeed lucky. If he became successful he could collect drawings, as did the painter, architect and historian, Giorgio Vasari in the Florence of the Renaissance, also Rembrandt and Rubens and, in England, Sir Joshua Reynolds and Sir Thomas Lawrence. He could haunt the art dealers and visit the printshops to take his material at second hand.

What is certain is that to further his personal education and learn his craft, he

9. Rembrandt, *The Artist drawing from a Model*; Unfinished etching, *c.* 1648

had to gain the necessary access to the work of other and preferably more skilled and more experienced draughtsmen. The most readily available and the most natural source of this material was the work of his contemporaries, and the greater those contemporaries were, the more fruitful was his inspiration and the better his education.

The coming of the Second World War, because it shut down the great museum collections, shut one off from their contents. It took one back into the position of one's predecessors. True, I had contemporaries – my elders and betters – who were of great value to me, but except in landscape-drawing I do not think I benefited as directly from them as perhaps I might have. I had some books of reproductions and just as artists in the past had had recourse to prints, these reproductions served my continuing apprenticeship. They did not, of course, give me the physical life an original achieves – and I mean physical.

Apart from its intellectual and formal qualities, drawing is an intensely physical activity and I am not sure how often people who don't draw, recognize how clearly those physical factors are revealed in drawings. For instance, in drawing *Hercules standing on Discord* (12) Rubens utilized copies he made while in Italy of the famous Antique statue called the *Farnese Hercules*. He is here making a drawing of a marble serve as the model for a painting. This drawing is not so much a copy as an adaptation. He is changing Hercules to make him labour differently, to make him stand on Discord. He has modified the position of the left leg several times. To establish the pose he has drawn the front of the thorax through the right arm. He has been very uncertain about how to place the arm holding the club.

This process of feeling his way is to be expected and is a private matter; it is Rubens's problem. The drawing shows him working at it. What can I read of the physical action – not the action of Hercules, but of Rubens? It is this. Firstly, his hand has moved fast. There is speed in the touch of the chalk, especially in those final commitments of the line such as the contours running abruptly down both legs. These were made after most of the modelling had been felt for, shaped and then established. Those strong contours are the signs of a man who, having made up his mind, strikes hard and sure. Those heavy lines eclipse the tentative, questioning lines which propose earlier alterations for the pose of the legs. These alternative statements are by no means evidence that Rubens did not know how to draw. The form is stated knowledgeably; the bulk of the shoulders and the twist of the trunk. The heel of his hand has not touched the paper, because chalk smudges. The movement of his wrist was all important. Except when he placed the accents, his fingers would have been relatively relaxed. The accents, in the eyes, under the nose, on the left draped forearm and right leg, are the result of hard-clamped fingers and strong pressure on the chalk tip. But the degree of pressure on the chalk would have been nothing like as heavy as Rembrandt's hand behind the reed or quill pen he had cut for himself, when he came to deliberate the composition of an etching which, in fact, he never finished (9). Drawing and incomplete etching demonstrate the procedure of his thought. In contrast to Rubens, the movement of Rembrandt's hand is here a matter of finger control and pressure and not of wrist movement. Every-thing comes out of the tension created between the finger-tips and the opposed thumb and this is true of his etchings where the touch, however black the resultant line, is very light indeed. Etching requires precision, but the steel needle point which delicately scratches away the thin wax ground on the copper to expose the line to the acid can be as light as a feather. Those dense blacks – and no other medium can give such stygian darks as etching – come from re-peated cross-hatching to build the shadows, touch by touch. It is the acid that

10. Mantegna, *The Calumny of Apelles*; Pen and brown ink, *c.* 1504 (*above*)

11. Rembrandt, *Copy after Mantegna's 'Calumny of Apelles'*; Pen and brown ink, *c.* 1655 (*below*)

does the strong work for, where it can get through the wax to the copper, where the metal is exposed by the hair-thin drawn line, it eats into it, creating incisions which will eventually hold the ink. Copper engraving is another matter. It needs controlled physical strength because the implements used are little razor-sharp gouges which directly and forcefully cut the line into the metal. It is laborious and precise. There is no easy method of correcting an error, which brings me back finally to where I started – to Albrecht Dürer.

I come back to him here, rather as I have come back to him personally after a quarter of a century of my neglect, not because he touches me deeply at an emotional level, but because, increasingly I have come to understand the kind of mind he had, and I am awed by it.

The famous drawing, *Apollo* (4), is an engraver's drawing, slowly, laboriously and minutely wrought with a sharp pen. Even the name of the god, inscribed

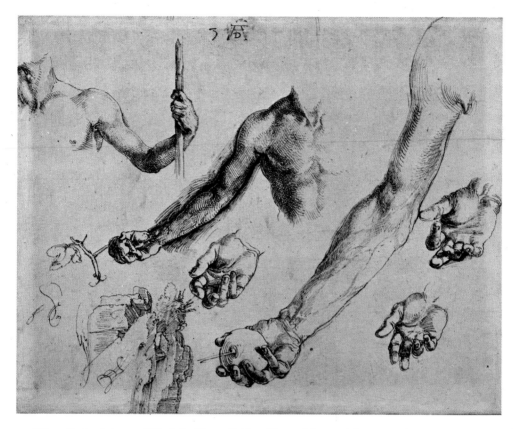

13. Dürer, *Study of Arms and Hands for Figure of Adam*; Pen and brown ink, *c.* 1504

and misspelt in the disc of the sun, is drawn backwards so that transferred to the copper plate, it will print in reverse and read the right way round. It is an abso-lutely Classical nude, the pose and form taken from the *Apollo Belvedere*, a Roman marble copy of a now lost Greek bronze original and perhaps the most famous of all Antique sculptures. Dürer took his source from a print of the statue, using it, as Rubens used the *Farnese Hercules*, for his own purposes. Three years later, reversing the stance of Apollo once more, he engraved on copper his famous *Fall of Adam* (5) and Apollo becomes Adam. One of the drawings I first held in my hands in the Print Room, when I was twelve years old, was a study for Adam's arms (13). It has haunted me ever since. In a way it is to me, the epitome of the drawing to learn from and also a lesson about originality and imitation, meaning and representation, inspiration and skill, private thought and public statement. Adam is here derived from a drawing, taken from another drawing, made after a print of a marble copy of a lost Greek bronze. Thus are the visual arts transmitted by imitation across time. But consider his arms. They demonstrate with superhuman clarity and with never a hesitant stroke, alternative possibilities as to exactly how those arms should be in the final picture. What began as a copy of a copy of a copy is here being transmuted. There are three arms on the paper and three different, separate hands. The artist here takes possession of his subject; the copies have served their purpose. In the engraving, all is once more reversed so that Adam's left arm in the drawing is to become his right in the engraving. The hand loosely grasps a pole which, in the engraving will become the branch of a tree. All the remaining studies are for the other hand and arm. Each is an exploration of a minute but vital problem. The problem is how do the human fingers most naturally hold an apple? How should it be got right?

Now if you look at your own hand holding an apple and turn it about, you will see that the slightest movement of your fingers will reshape, to your eyes, the physical relationship of each digit to the others, the tension across the knuckles, the slack of the palm, the geometry of the bones. There are a hundred subtle possibilities for variations, for new drawings, before your eyes. Should you come to engrave it or cut it in marble, or cast it in bronze or paint it, there will be one chosen solution: one solution that seems *right* in the context. This drawing shows us Dürer looking privately for that solution. The drawing is private, the engraving is public. And ironically, in the engraving, the apple has not reached Adam's hand. Eve and the serpent still hold it.

What the drawing gives us because it is private, that the engraving does not because it is public, is an intimate, immediate indication of Dürer's mind at work; selecting, discarding, probing for the answer he needed. In contemplating such a drawing you are admitted into the process of visual thought and you will be, while you look at it, briefly not only at the centre of a great artist's mind, but in the spontaneous movement of his hand. You are watching him create the illusion of three dimensions, of sculptural form on a flat surface. You are watching him marshal his experience of looking not only at the human hand but, behind that, at all the works of art he had conscientiously studied during his life in order to do it.

It may be because the hand is my own instrument, obedient so far as I can make it, to my eye and to my mind, that these hands of Dürer's are so significant. They are no ordinary hands. But then it is no ordinary apple he sought to make the hand grasp. It is in the most particular sense the fruit of the tree of knowledge.

Chapter Four

The Egyptians

Fleur Cowles

Beautiful archaeological objects have always fascinated me and their survival amazes me even more. The reconstruction of the past seems to me to be a mystical and magical experience, particularly Egypt's past, a glittering story that covers a span of 4000 years of human experience. No one will ever see all the Egyptian relics that do exist, or are yet to be dug out of the sand, but at the British Museum we can view an almost unrivalled collection, and for that we are privileged.

The country's rare climate and its rare and ancient rituals account for the scale, almost unmatched of the discoveries made in the Nile Valley. The Egyptians deliberately and lovingly buried their treasures in ceremonies connected with death – which, as a means to yet another life ahead – was treated with ceremonial jubilation. Thus, much still remains.

Before the First Dynasty, Egyptians simply buried their dead in shallow trenches, the bodies being preserved by desiccation in the hot, dry sand. When, about 3000 B.C., the nobility started building super-structures over the sand, destruction of some of the contents began. Still, when one uncovers a tomb, much inside is miraculously intact, unharmed.

Tombs were sometimes plundered and pillaged, but were not otherwise damaged; everything found is in a natural state of preservation and in a perfect storehouse. Even a few hundred miles to the north, in Greece or Italy, much would have perished.

Imagine the thrill of opening a royal tomb sealed thousands of years ago. Perhaps that of a queen, buried with so much finery, with all her favourite possessions, even her pets! In the intervening thousands of years she has lain there undisturbed, her possessions untouched, and so often even her name forgotten. And yet today, as we walk casually through the Egyptian galleries of the British Museum and see laid out before us so many aspects of such a monarch's life, even her mummified body, we walk straight back in time and can, if we use a little imagination and take the trouble to observe carefully what we see, re-create numerous fascinating details of the life she led.

This I do when I visit the Egyptian rooms at the British Museum. Egyptology is not my forte, nor am I an art historian, but it gives me great pleasure to write about the things I love, even if, in this particular case, doing so makes me long for the erudition of a Robert Graves, or of an Egyptologist.

When I think of those rooms, half my heart is tilted in memory of days spent in Egypt in the early 1950s, when I wandered, exhausted and bewildered, round the abundant jumble of beauty of the Tutankhamen relics in the Cairo Museum. Visiting archaeological sites, (Greek and Arab and Persian, as well as Egyptian ruins) has been a luxury I've enjoyed for the last twenty years of restless travel, and each experience of the relics of other civilizations has been enriching.

Working my way from one floor to the next of the British Museum's Egyptian world is like being on a dream-walk: here a snake encrusted in gems, and everywhere lotuses, carved, painted and jewelled, abloom on tomb, on mummy, on papyri, on paintings, and on gems; eels and crocodiles mummified and buried with the pomp of the nobles they accompanied; the birds caught in the paw of a cat retriever (dogs were not then used as such); gold flowing like water, spilling over the images of nobles; imperturbable gods with heads of falcon, or cobra, or bird, or cat; court records of thieves (like modern ones, but in that period written in hieroglyphics on papyri); jewels of devastating beauty; titanic statues and a massive bronze scarab.

To use, such things seem almost unreal, but to the ancient Egyptians they were the customary symbols, the ordinary artifacts and the routine gods, of day-to-day life. And they are all very beautiful. As an artist myself, and as a woman, I find their splendour irresistible and the images they evoke endlessly delightful. Sometimes, I think of these rooms as a woman's world – especially when looking at painted gardens, exquisite furniture, artisans carved in wood, beautiful little seated queens or giant mummies painted and decorated with women's masks (their cosmetic ideas not one bit foreign to our own day and age). And what woman could possibly overlook all those feline pets?

Long ago, to simplify my visits, I made myself a breakdown of the three main divisions within this ancient civilization that interested me most. Then, as I wander through the collections, I fit what I see into a personal pattern. As long as I bear it in mind I am not bewildered by the thousands of miscellaneous objects that however carefully set out and explained are not easy to piece together. Though it has taken time, I have now found a place for most things: not by dynasty, year or place, but according to its purpose and use in the scheme of ancient Egyptian society.

First of all, life itself. For all those thousands of years, it was lived with a haunting reverence for a large number of gods, mostly in animal form. When I see a stone falcon over a man's head, I know that the men of those times saw it as a representation of Horus, the sky god.

Secondly, death. With what extravagance it was met, and how fascinating the ritual of mummification (which I shall later describe in its gory detail).

Thirdly, the obsession with after-life. Egyptians expected to live again and for this reason they were entombed with objects they expected to use after death. Each elegant piece of furniture, each sheet of papyrus with its mysterious symbols, each exquisite wall-painting, each tribute to a god, each jewel in a case (all came from these tombs) tells of their plans for an after-life appropriate to the status they had enjoyed on earth.

In each category, I have gleaned as much knowledge as I need for my pleasure – and, in every case, I've finally arrived at my favourite examples. In the limited space given to me, I shall do my best to describe them.

Life

One must begin by describing the ancient Egyptian: he was intelligent and gentle, he loved his family and friends, he loved gaiety and the good life, he had a sense of humour and an absorbing delight in work and administration.

One must also summarize his efforts during the thousands of years of recorded history when giant steps were taken towards the standards of civilization we now enjoy. Irrigation was controlled, new metals found and used, animals domesti-cated, monumental architecture evolved, writing invented (leaving us superb historical records), and the first commercial organizations developed and docu-mented. The Egyptian's technical skill was amazing – in stone-carving, in weaving, in cabinet-making, in the working of metals, in shipbuilding, in mining. As a jeweller, his work was unrivalled until medieval times.

And all this occurred in a Nile Valley which was both ribbon of mud and a spreading delta. Through thousands of years, a tradition persisted. Egyptian culture kept its style and character quite unsullied by the ideas and customs of most of the rest of mankind.

Although humans have given special treatment to animals for 100,000 years (starting in caves and ending as jewels) animal-deity worship began before the fourth millennium, when men on the Nile grouped into tribes, each with its own god. This was generally an animal or a bird, but gradually these beasts gave up their own bodies to become hybrid-humans, keeping only the head of one or the other to place on the other's body. The transition was so smooth, one can even look now at a goddess with an ape's snout without shock.

Men worshipped any force, even a baby snake, if they thought it exercised a special influence for good or prevented harm. If an animal was feared, from that fear followed worship. The wandering Egyptian regarded the deadly snake and crocodile as sacred as soon as he believed worship would provide protection.

1. Mummified cats, from cats' cemeteries, sacred to the cat goddess Bastet

Divine status thus went to many animals, and ultimately they were mummified to go into the burial-grounds with the bodies of kings.

My favourite among these animals is the cat goddess, Bastet (usually represented by a woman with a cat's head). The actual animal species had upright ears, fur of a brownish-grey colour, a white underbelly, the body sometimes streaked or striped in black and ochre, its length about two and a half feet, its tail long. It was variously used, not only as a retriever in hunting but as man's first mousetrap. From the granary it was a short walk to the foot of a throne. The animal soon rose from the lowly position of a local deity to one of the great divinities of Egypt. Wild cats were domesticated – admired for their virility, ferocity and agility – and soon became all-popular, although they never achieved the status of a royal goddess.

If a fire started in a house, for instance, the death of the family cat would be the most painful loss. To kill one (or a falcon or an ibis) meant death, often at the hands of neighbours before the trial took place. Mothers often gave their daughters a name which meant 'little cat'.

The cat was a goddess of pleasure. She loved music; she loved to dance and in an emergency she could be relied upon to ward off contagious diseases. One of the most celebrated and orgiastic of all festivals celebrated in Egypt was in her honour, a huge animal fair at her temple at Bubastis (once described in detail by Herodotus after a visit from Greece). Worshippers arrived by barge to the sound of castanets, walked in splendid processions to the sound of tumultuous cheering and in an atmosphere of buffoonery and high spirits. Wine flowed freely.

More statues seem to have been dedicated to Bastet than to any other god: countless examples are in the Museum, in stone, in clay, jewelled, painted and mummified. All cats were, of course, carefully buried after a life of veneration.

There were huge cat cemeteries all over Egypt. And even the mummified cat (1) sometimes had the use at death of the same god who presided over humans.

This god was *Anubis* – a *black jackal* which had become the god of death. As Lord of the Mummy Wrapping, Anubis invented all funeral rites and the art of embalming. Funeral prayers were addressed exclusively to him. The sleek, black animal always took the human dead by the hand to the presence of the sovereign judges where the dead man's soul could be weighed.

Horus, the god of the sky was *falcon-headed* (2). Like the bird soaring and dipping in the sky, he seemed to be the sky itself – a pre-eminently divine being. A

2. Horus in the guise of a falcon

curious division of the sexes is applied to all the solar gods; Horus was male, the earth was male (Geb), the moon, male (Thoth), the sky was female – and how was she represented? As a cow! She was called Hathor.

Another sky goddess was human in form. Called Nut, she was usually portrayed as a nude woman whose long, arched body touched the earth at tiptoes and finger-tips. What men saw shining in the night was really her star-studded belly.

The lady lion was singled out for multiple attributes. *Sekhmet*, 'the terrible lioness-headed woman', was goddess of war and battle, full of vengeance. She was once thought to have intended to exterminate the entire human race. Her terribleness also included responsibility for fire (she could even devour the fire of the sun).

Egypt must be the only place on earth that ever worshipped a *crocodile*. *Sebek* is either seen in its own hideous likeness or as a man with the head of a crocodile. Some provinces hunted the reptile down and destroyed it, others worshipped it (with fratricidal wars to decide the issue). It was obviously fearsome enough to be appeased as a god; some were even given golden ear-rings to wear, others had gold bracelets riveted to forelegs. There was even a special sanctuary for them (*Crocodilopolis*) where they could live in splendour. Then, as today, they became tourist attractions.

One legend is amusing: King Menes (probably the first King of Egypt) was supposed to have been attacked by his own dogs but saved by a crocodile, who

3. Scarab; incarnation of the god Khepri; black granite

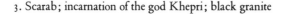

4. Commemorative scarabs issued by Amenhetep III; c. 1417–1379 B.C.

carried him to the other shore of a lake. *Crocodilopolis* was supposedly built by the King in gratitude.

The *scarab-beetle* god, *Khepri*, is linked with two functions: one, as the amulet used to protect a dead man's heart in the embalming process – when the scarab god was placed on the breast, to give the body a new source of life and movement after death; the other, to prevent the valued physical heart (which was thought to be the seat of the emotions) from speaking against the dead man.

Worship of the beetle came from its extraordinary habit of burying its eggs in balls of dung, which were rolled along between its legs, giving the newborn larvae something to feed on. The Egyptians identified the scarab with the power behind the sun – which rolled in similar fashion across the sky much as the ball of eggs encased in dung rolled across the sand. From this activity, Khepri was considered to be the source of power (indeed, given credit for rolling the ball of sun into the Other World each evening and back again each morning, representing the renewal of life and the idea of eternal existence). He was also considered to be the god of existence, which the name *Khepri* means.

The importance of placing a scarab as an amulet on a dead body to give potential life was obvious. Such amulets of scarabs are found in thousands of varieties. Eventually, the habit of the living to wear one as an ornament came into modern fashion – and it eventually became a royal emblem (certainly of the last Farouk).

The colossal scarab seen in the Museum's Sculpture Gallery (3) comes from a Constantinople temple, to which it was probably taken in Byzantine times. It is the largest in the world. (By contrast, you can see in the Jewel Room, a tiny scarab gem in a rich clear blue glass.)

Under King Amenhetep III, an issue of scarabs (4) was designed to commemorate events he considered historic. Some are extremely rare, but the British Museum has assembled the entire collection. The events commemorated range from the King's marriages, to the giving of gifts to his Queens, to the number of lions or cattle he killed, to the digging of a pleasure lake for his chief Queen at Zarukha (a colossal feat, dug in seventy days)! Though tiny, each scarab tells the whole story.

Another Museum scarab has a special history. Rumours of a theft had been reported thousands of years ago. A court of inquiry had been appointed. The thieves were captured and their confessions recorded on papyri – they admitted stealing the scarab in one tomb and dropping it in another. In the Museum we can see the scarab and the papyri which record the story.

Now we come to a remarkable bird, the *Ibis*, which was sacred to Thoth. It was credited by the Egyptians with hatching the world from an egg. This was done with the help of the four gods and four goddesses whom he produced from sounds made by his own voice. Together, the nine created the world and later, the Ibis was credited with developing manifold talents: he invented hieroglyphics, he was the seat of learning and he was the scribe of the gods. Thoth's wife was her husband's 'shadow' or 'double', known as the 'Mistress of the House of Books'.

It was somehow decided that the hippopotamus was a female. *Thoeris* is always seen as a long-breasted beast, nearly always standing upright and always heavy with child (5). My favourite example in the Museum is a small hippopotamus in rich, clear blue glass, but another in the Sculpture Gallery – a large red and yellow statue, is also striking.

Heqet was a lady frog who represented the embryonic state between a living grain and its final germination, which took place when it decomposed. Thus, she too symbolized fertility, fecundity, birth, renewed life.

Even the vile scorpion was deified. *Selkis's* function was to protect the conjugal union (stinging the adulterer, no doubt)!

The bull *Apis*, is today's best-known sacred animal. Honoured through Egypt, he was always black and easily recognizable by certain mystic marks: a white triangle on his forehead, the figure of a vulture in flight on his back, a crescent moon on his right flank, a scarab on his tongue – and a tail with double hairs. He too had his own temple, from which he was let loose daily: like the crocodile, his presence in the courtyard made the temple a place of pilgrimage.

5. Thoeris, goddess of childbirth, represented as pregnant, female hippopotamus; faience

At Saqqarah, mummified bodies of huge bulls were found in vast subterranean chambers. Their burial had followed resplendent funerals on immense, monolithic sarcophagi. The sacred cows of Memphis also had their own vast catacombs.

Buto, the cobra (also called Edjo and Nadjet) deserves a chapter on its own, so complex is its place among the gods. In early times it was associated with fertility. Soon, fear became the overwhelming obsession. In order to keep snakes away, emblems of the cobra were put on much of the furniture. Believing in magic, they thought that by throwing a boomerang round a bed – thereby marking out a particular territory – no snake would dare cross the line. Because of its evil power, the snake was a sign of sovereignty and royalty.

Snakes were also worn as charms and jewels, and snake-amulets were always buried near the dead along with mummified cobras. Buried in the earth – from which serpents came forth – the dead were especially exposed to danger. The coiled snake that once decorated the brow of royal statues is with us again in profusion: today, it appears as a jewel of sudden and somewhat inexplicable popularity.

Khnum, the ram-headed, is thought to have moulded man on a potter's wheel! But three other animal gods had the most thankless assignment of all: they (and a fourth, a human god) were protectors of the viscera of the dead. After removal from the corpse, these organs were always placed in four special jars (the so-

6. The so-called Canopic Jars showing from left to right, Hapi, baboon-headed; Duamutef, jackal-headed; Imsety, a human-headed god; and Qebhsenuef, who has a falcon head

called 'Canopic Jars' – (6)), with heads of different gods. A human god watched over the liver; Qebhsenuef, falcon-headed, over the intestines; *Hapi*, the baboon-headed, guarded the lungs; and Duamutef, who had a jackal's head, had charge of the stomach.

There are many other animal gods but I have mentioned those that are the most numerous in the Museum.

Death

Burial was of supreme importance. Life on the rich land was so full of good things that no man wanted an existence after death which did not contain an idyllic reconstruction of its best elements. Everything to ensure it went into a man's tomb.

If you were a king or a noble, in death as in life, you expected a fuller life than a mere commoner – and for this reason, all the best went into such graves. Whoever he was, every Egyptian aspired to continuity, but a tomb was a privilege. If a man was poor, he might be buried in the Nile. A nobleman wanted his name to survive, his body to remain intact and the food and drink he loved to be regularly supplied. Texts were left in each tomb to make certain of this. Drawings were also left so that, by some magic, the form of life so deftly illustrated would be carried on posthumously.

Preservation of the body (7) by embalming was so important for the after-life that it became one of the principal aims of funerary practice at a very early period. Removal of internal organs dates from the Fourth Dynasty.

Preparing the body for interment was a process which took seventy days, half of this time being devoted to drying the body after viscera and brain had been removed. That was one method. The other was to soak the body in a solution of natron and water. Only the heart, the seat of understanding, was left inside. Most of the brain was withdrawn through the nostrils with an iron hook; what was left was dissolved with lotions. Natron was used to dry the body, to dissolve fats and to leave the skin supple but not tender. After the viscera were removed, the abdomen was first washed with palm wine and then filled with crushed myrrh, cassia and other aromatics. Then the body was sewn up. Each finger and each toe was bandaged, then each limb and finally the whole body. A king's arms would be covered in jewels, his toes and fingers sheathed in gold. Across the waist and body, bits of gold and glazed beads and necklaces and daggers were placed. Tutankhamen's mummy is the most exquisite example anywhere.

Whatever organs were removed were treated with natron and buried in the animal-headed jars in the tomb itself. Often the body cavity was packed with linen (sometimes with sawdust or sand), then the incision was sewn up and covered with a plate of leather or metal. The eye of falcon-headed Horus was put over it for protection. Eye-sockets were plugged with wads of linen or given artificial eyes. The body was anointed, spiced and resined and then wrapped in a series of bandages not only to protect it but to build up the bulk and form of the deceased.

Sacred animals of appropriate protective genius were mummified and buried in their own cemeteries, with every effort made, as in humans, to produce a wrapped mummy that was convincing in appearance.

The Mummy Room, for me, is a sombre experience – so much beauty painted on the outside wrappings, but with all those human bones beneath. Yet, T.E. Lawrence once exclaimed about a certain mummy, 'This is the most beautiful thing I've ever seen!'

Afterlife

Simple people were buried with pottery, jugs, tools, utensils and even baskets of food and drink. Kings and nobles buried pieces of furniture, chests of clothing and all those other objects of value which such a person would not want to be without. Of particular importance were the tiny *shabti*-figures (later called *shawabtis* and *ushabtis*) which went into tombs to act as slaves and workers for the deceased (8). They were placed there to do the manual work that the Egyptians believed would be as necessary in the Underworld as it had been during life on earth: rehabilitating the land, irrigating it, carrying sand and stones in the building of dikes, cutting canals. Some *shabtis* were carved in wood or stone, but the majority were of faience.

A new papyrus, recently added to the Museum collection, is the only document of its kind. It is the original bill for a set of 401 *shabti*-figures buried with a nobleman: one for each day of the year plus thirty-six extras to act as foremen or overseers. This small bill of sale, five inches high by nine inches wide and consisting of ten lines of hieratic, just bought by the Museum is, in fact, the key which explains so much about the origin of these 401 figures – how they were obtained and the process by which magic was imparted to them. Egyptologists have wanted to know for a hundred years about the curious purchase of hundreds of figures by one man!

That green, fertile papyrus – how few other plants have played so dominant a role in the life, art and industry of a civilization! Tied together, stems of papyrus supported roofs of early houses. Later, they were replaced by carved stone replicas of an enormous scale to uphold roofs of great temples. Papyrus, bundled together, formed boats. The outer bark made crates, baskets and even furniture.

8. A shabti of Amenhetep III

9. Fowling in a marsh; fresco from the tomb of Nebamun; *c.* 1400 B.C.; XVIIIth dynasty

And from the pith of the stems came the writing-paper for the scrolls.

Papyrus coffin-texts insured a good life and also gave the dead the power to leave the tomb when necessary. Among those displayed in the Museum is the first insurance policy in the world, a document belonging to a Crown Prince and guaranteeing him protection against accidental illness or harm. A priest would have been the broker, no doubt enjoying a lucrative sideline. Another tomb-papyrus is the oldest mathematical treatise, telling how to calculate the volume of a pyramid. The oldest crossword puzzle on earth is there – or is it an acrostic? – dated about 1100 B.C.

Of the painted frescoes which decorated the tombs of noblemen, the most beautiful in the Museum are somewhat hidden in an upper room by a corridor of displays: I urge you to go behind to see them. One, '*In the Garden*', is an ex-quisitely painted window on nature: rows of trees are set out in a square, surrounding a pool in which fish, birds and lilies live in poetic harmony. Two geese are walking, instead of swimming, on the water.

Another lovely painting is a fowling scene (9) for which there must be a magical explanation. The hunter is tossing the serpent-boomerang which represents the destruction of evil forces. The boomerang flies at a bird, stuns it, and a light-footed cat leaps high to retrieve it as it falls. The colouring and composition is playful and gay.

Other wall-frescoes show scenes indicating taxation reports. In one, cattle are counted (their humped backs showing their Asian origin). In another, geese are lined up in such profusion and with such elegance, one gasps in admiration. In most, one finds the nobleman watching the exercise, and usually also the scribe who is there to record it. The lovely bearded wheat in these ancient frescoes still grows in Egypt today.

*   *   *

The Egyptian's greatest contribution to world culture was his art, characterized by great dignity, an exquisite sense of design and colour, and impeccable taste. Painters in those days had to give a maximum view of everything they represented, to tie in with the day's acceptance of magic. In their mixed thinking, they painted faces only in profile and bodies only in front view (as in a beautiful banquet scene on a wall-painting from a tomb in Thebes). All but two girl musicians are in profile, in the stiff, stylized manner of the day. Each profiled head has one eye staring straight at the viewer, as, for example, in Picasso. In the same lovely scene, the painter bravely flaunted innovation by showing two maidens full face, instead of in the required profile, and by painting the dancers with bodies in profile. He also showed shadows under their toes – an unusual touch of realism. Sculptors had other traditions: they carved ears, for instance, so that one could see the full ear from the front view. Kings, being gods and never mere mortals, were always sculptured dead straight and head on, totally immobile, imprisoned in a rigid style. Only an occasional face shows an unexpected dose of realism, solemn but not pompous, serious but never sad. Royal dignity required no rich garment or lavish dress. Though looking at nearly naked men, we know we are in the presence of kings. One is overwhelmed by the solemnity of royal portraits. Men were kings mainly by hereditary privilege. All are impressive.

The Sculpture Gallery is an amazing experience. Starting with the huge coffins, one then comes upon the Rosetta Stone, about which a book could be written, then the colossus of the Shabaka Stone. The large, recumbent lions were picked by Ruskin as 'the noblest and truest carved lions I have ever seen. And

yet, in them, the lions' manes and beards are represented by rings of solid rock
as smooth as a mirror.' These lions are of artistic importance because one was
completed by King Amenhetep III for a temple in Nubia (10), then captured
and carried away by an Ethiopian king a thousand years later. When recaptured,
a second was finished in Tutankhamen's time and carried back to Nubia.

On the other end of the art spectrum, we find a folk-art in the tombed possessions of simple, poorer people. These are the free and unfettered records of the
human conditions of their time. There were so many musical instruments, they
must have dearly loved music (but no one has been able to reproduce what they
played – there is no key). They loved games. Draught-boards and even a sort of
parchesi and backgammon were found – even a 'snakes and ladders' carved in
stone – with a snake actually forming the pattern. We can see wooden figures
demonstrating wine being made, bread being baked (loaves of bread 3500 years
old were found at Thebes), men making beer (the brewery ranked second only to
the granary and the bakery – and depended on both); eels were fished for, men
sailed boats and made sandals.

I have often watched women gallery visitors. They always try to locate the
things of cosmetic value to the fabled Egyptian beauties (inspired no doubt by
Cleopatra films). For genuine evidence we go back to the objects found in
tombs. Perfumes and cosmetics were once so costly they were sometimes stolen
in preference to gold. One tomb (Tutankhamen's), twice invaded, lost gold and
gems the first time round. Next time, gems and gilt were left behind for the valuable oils and cosmetic ingredients stolen instead and poured into leather gourds
for removal. Over a century later, stolen tubes of *kohl* (eye-paint) from this very
grave were found in another tomb. The original oily fingerprints are still visible
on the leather gourds.

Perfume, as we understand it, did not then exist; distillation processes were
not yet developed. All smell is gone and no analysis can be made of what they
might have used but if we look at the paintings, royal women are using perfumes
of some sort and ancient tools of beauty just as now. In the room with the jewels
are highly polished bronze mirrors and also sticks to help a woman apply rouge
to cheek and lips.

Women used oils in great quantity then, often placing little cones of scented
fat on top of their heads to melt in the heat and trickle over face and body!
Women hennaed their hair and also painted their nails and hands with the same
dye. A few years ago, when I attended a secret nuptial ceremony in the Hadh-
ramout in South Arabia, the hennaed thirteen-year-old bride was having her
nails and hands painted by her attendants precisely as we believe the ancient
Egyptians did.

If one looks at the masks over queens' coffins, no further evidence is needed

10. The Prudhoe Lion sculpted for the tomb of Amenhetep III; red granite

of the importance of eye make-up: blue-glass paste, like lapis lazuli, encircle eyes, the sort of skilful use of colour which must have been every beautiful woman's aim. The make-up was kept in little jars and applied with little ebony sticks.

If one wonders why jewellery was all so lavish (11 and 12), it is because its use was restricted to kings and their families, or to priests and functionaries of the Court. Most of these gems, as far as I am concerned, defy written or even photo-graphic description; the combination of colour plus texture plus scale gives so much to the eye.

Very often jewels were made in the shape of petals, flowers, bells, lotus pods, fish – the beautiful elements of everyday life. But often they were animal gods and abstract forms (like a certain T-shape, of special meaning). The colours mainly represented the earth, greenery, sky and sea. They were mainly made in stone, otherwise in glaze, sometimes in cloisonné.

At first, only a blue or a green colour could be achieved in a glaze, the colours that came from a copper base. Artists today might note their canny use of blue; it is always there because the Egyptians knew the impact of the colour even in tiny doses. Later, the art of glazing was brilliantly perfected and we see purple-blue, violet, livid apple-green, bright chrome- and lemon-yellows, crimson and brownish reds, and even chalk-white. All artists benefited.

Silver, called 'white gold', was in many ways a favourite as it was thought to be the metal of the sun they worshipped. Gold became plentiful for the use of royalty after the Nubian mines came under Egyptian control. To see these pieces today is to realize how incorruptible gold is, how endowed with permanence.

Faience, made of powdered quartz, and lime, and natron (of embalming fame), was covered with alkaline glaze to make beads. A splendid job of imitating lapis lazuli was also achieved. Precious stones were not 'home-grown': real lapis lazuli came from Afghanistan; emeralds came from Upper Egypt, in very limited supply; turquoise came from the Sinai or Arabia; crystal and amethysts from the wadis of southern Egypt; obsidian and volcanic glass from Ethiopia.

But the real beauty lay in the simple objects into which they were fashioned. Such creativity and taste surely influenced art for centuries – and continues to inspire us, even today.

11. Necklace of gold and carnelian beads, and gold earrings; New Kingdom; c. 1200 B.C. (*above*)

12. Blue faience beads and amulets (hawks, and figures of Ptah, the patron of artisans and artists); XVIIIth dynasty; c. 1400 B.C. (*below*)

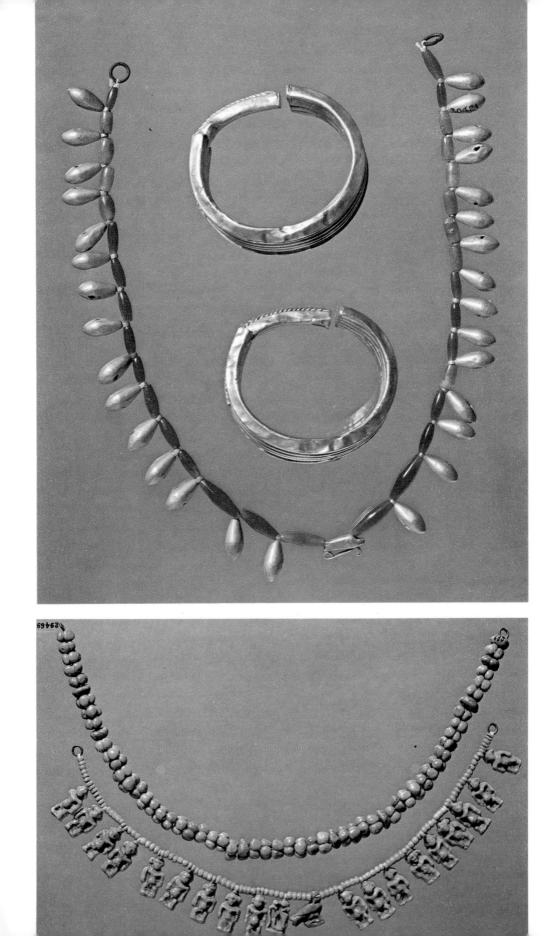

Chapter Five

The Greeks

Tyrone Guthrie

The Elgin Marbles are some of the finest works of art ever shaped in stone. They are a series of sculptures; a frieze in marble relief which came originally from the Parthenon in Athens. They are also the crown of the British Museum's Greek collection.

To understand their significance we must look back to Athens as it was 400 years before the birth of Christ when the city was at the height of its glory. At that time it was not the capital of Greece but the most important of several Greek city states, each of them independent politically and economically, but united by a common language and close ties of religion, history and culture. Athens acquired its leading role after playing a major part in the defeat of the Persian invaders (500–449 B.C.). In the Age of Pericles, and in the century that followed, she enjoyed her greatest period of intellectual, artistic and political activity. The Parthenon was built, sculpture flourished, and philosophers like Anaxagoras and Socrates, and dramatists such as Aeschylus, Sophocles and Euripides created the Athenian art and institutions which have had a predominant influence on what has come to be called 'Western' thought and imagination.

Towards the end of the fifth century B.C. Athens was involved in a long-drawn-out war with Sparta, another city state. Sparta was victorious in a struggle which exhausted both cities physically, financially and morally. And what is Sparta now? A scattered hamlet with no tangible sign of its former glory – no art, no literature, nothing but the legend of its victory, which has, ironically, survived as a part of Athenian history.

Perhaps the greatest single monument to Athenian civilization is the Parthenon, begun in 450 B.C. and dedicated in 438 B.C. It is the work of Phidias, one of the greatest of the Greek artists and possibly the greatest of all artists in stone of any age. He was appointed by Pericles to superintend the adornment of Athens, and the Parthenon was erected as a temple for Athene, goddess of wisdom and patron deity of Athens. Phidias suffered a harsh reward for his efforts. He was accused of introducing Pericles and his own likeness on the shield of the goddess and he died in prison.

The Parthenon, erected on the Acropolis, dominates the city. It is a gigantic edifice of matchless architectural proportion which took some fourteen years to

Bronze head of Apollo,
from Tamassus, Cyprus;
Greek; *c.* 460 B.C.

Clay toilet box with lid
(pyscis) on which stand
four horses;
Attic Geometric,
760–740 B.C.

build. During its history it has served many gods. In the fifth century the building was used as a Christian church. In the fifteenth century it became a Turkish mosque. It has not survived unscathed though most of the damage is man-made. The worst of it occurred in 1687 when Venetian cannon bombarded an occupy-ing force of Turks and a great explosion destroyed the roof and much of the sides.

The Elgin Marbles, the work of Phidias and his fellow craftsmen, are frag-ments, some taken from the fabric of the Parthenon, others salvaged from its ruins. The panels, each about three feet by four, once formed a frieze which ran round the tops of the columns supporting the temple. They represent a procession which one can view almost like a strip cartoon, following it from one end to the other right round the vast rectangle of the colonnade.

I am not going to say that to the uninstructed eye the frieze is immediately beautiful and interesting. It is not one of those sights which evoke instinctive and primitive reactions of awe and pleasure. But then, reaction to great works of art is far less primitive and more intellectual, and one cannot expect to appreciate them just as easily as one can enjoy the sight of a basket of kittens or a great four-masted sailing-ship. Many people never get further than liking what they think they ought to like. So-called 'popular' art (and I don't mean 'Pop' art) consists entirely of currently acceptable and popular images of beauty.

There are several reasons why the Elgin Marbles are not in this category. For one thing they are considerably damaged; many of the panels lay on the ground for years after they crashed from the top of the colonnade. For another, they are now colourless, whereas originally they, and the temple as a whole, were brilliantly and realistically coloured. Finally, they are enormously elaborate and detailed which means they are barely intelligible to a visitor who allocates to them no more than a casual glance, unless the visitor is aware of who and what is illustrated.

Apart from the panels which make up the frieze, the Elgin Marbles include several groups of statuary, much larger than life-size, which originally decorated the pediment or gable of the Parthenon. Judging by their proportions and their dominant position in the architectural and decorative scheme, we can infer that they represent deities of great importance. But it is no longer possible to be certain because the remains are too fragmentary.

These statues are considered by those who know a great deal more than I to be absolute masterpieces. I can't see them except as mutilated objects which perhaps one might appreciate if they were whole. But it ill becomes ignorance to be other than humble. Let us accept them as masterpieces and be grateful that even so much has been preserved.

Grateful to whom? Well, in the first place to the seventh Earl of Elgin who has given his name to the collection. He was British Ambassador to Turkey at the

Bronze head of a griffin from the rim of a cauldron; probably found in Rhodes; Greek, c. 650 B.C.

Hermes (left), herald and messenger of the gods, distinguished by his traveller's boots, cloak and hat. Dionysus (right), god of wine; Elgin Marbles, East Frieze

time when Greece was under Turkish domination. About 1800 he visited Athens and finding that unparalleled works of art were in danger of being destroyed, he set himself the task of acquiring the treasures and removing them to England. Shortly after the completion of his mission the British Treasury compensated Elgin for the £35,000 he had spent and the Marbles became the property of the nation.

A contemporary caricature in the British Museum shows us the popular reaction to the purchase. John Bull is angrily remonstrating with Milord at being compelled to pay money for stones, when his children need bread. Subsequently, criticism of Elgin centred on the argument that Britain had no right to take possession of the artistic achievements of poorer countries. In fairness to Elgin it should be remembered that the Marbles, many of which were already severely damaged, would almost certainly have been destroyed if they had remained in Athens until the end of Turkish rule. Some of the statues that remained were in fact ground down to make cement.

Of course, this danger no longer exists. Now it is argued that if the British Government were to return the Marbles to Greece they could not be replaced on the Parthenon but would merely be set up in another museum where they would be seen by fewer people than they are today. But if we pursue this line of reasoning

Heifers led to sacrifice. The cords by which they were held were represented either by bronze or by painting; Elgin Marbles, South Frieze (*opposite above*)

Horsemen in procession, Elgin Marbles, North Frieze (*opposite below*)

to its logical conclusion, all the most interesting and beautiful products of human artifice must be centralized in a very few huge museums, colossally endowed by the wealthiest communities who can ensure that the treasures are safely housed and splendidly displayed.

Suppose that, during the next 500 years, the artistic achievements of humanity were to be collected into four stupendous museums, say, Kansas City, Leningrad, Peking and Melbourne. Wouldn't it be rather hard on cities like Paris, Vienna, Munich or London to be forced to sell their treasures, and be deprived of a considerable and growing tourist revenue and, still more, of their contribution to the general enrichment of the native scene? Moreover, isn't there something rather dull about collections so vast as to overwhelm visitors? In my view, even the National Gallery in London, or the Louvre, or the Metropolitan Museum of Art in New York, would be much more enjoyable, as well as more comprehensible, if far fewer pictures were to be seen; if they were split into several smaller collections. I think there is a great deal to be said for an international fund for the return of works of art to points as close as possible to the places where they were created. Meanwhile, let us be thankful to people like Lord Elgin who, perhaps because they were fortunately placed well above the line of mere economic survival, were able to take long views.

The British Museum collection should, among other things, teach us also to take the long view. There is a room in the Greek section in which every object is over 3000 years old. You might say that mere antiquity is not necessarily of very great significance. It is easy to imagine, for instance, some modern thing of no great artistic value surviving, by a lucky accident, another thousand years; a beer-barrel, say, stored under a buttress of some immensely deep and strong cellar. But what might seem to us, its contemporaries, a perfectly ordinary object could not fail to be of surpassing interest to our distant successors. The materials would be studied and expert assessments published ('It is made of wood, a material derived from trees which in those days covered wide tracts of the world's surface, and it is ingeniously shaped and bound by hoops made of what they used to call iron'). There would be speculation as to its use. It would throw some tiny light on the great darkness which by then would have descended upon twentieth-century civilization.

Now suppose the passage of another 2000 years and the inevitable loss of antiquities during this period through destruction and decay. I hold it to be almost inconceivable that survival for so long could be just a matter of chance, like the beer-barrel under a buttress. The things which survive will have been deliberately preserved; precious objects in an air-tight box in a fireproof vault; objects chosen for preservation because they inspire reverence and affection. This is why a wise man does not look at a very ancient relic in a spirit of trivial

Clay drinking-cup (*kylix*), from Camirus Rhodes; Aphrodite riding on a goose; painted by the Pistoxenos Painter; Attic, *c.* 460 B.C. (*above*)

Bronze figure of a warrior on horseback; from Lucania; Greek, *c.* 550 B.C. (*below*)

Marble statue of Demeter, from Cnidus in Asia Minor; Greek; *c.* 330 B.C. (*left*)

Marble figure of a woman, from Amorgos; 2800–2500 B.C. (*right*)

curiosity. To have survived at all it must once have been very precious. A high
proportion of British Museum exhibits were objects that were highly valued by
the Greeks because they were connected with religion. The Greeks were a god-
haunted people. Wherever he was and whatever he was doing, the fifth-century
Athenian felt himself to be in the invisible but awe-inspiring presence of a deity.

He acquired most of his theological ideas from Homer who has been described
as 'the first and the greatest of European poets'. Homer preceded the great days
of Classical Athens by four centuries but he was thought to enshrine all wisdom
and knowledge and the *Iliad* and the *Odyssey* were the basis of Greek education
and cultural life. In fact, these epic poems were the Bible of the Greeks.

The Homeric concept of religion was founded on the concept of a great family

Multiple clay vase, perhaps for offerings; *c.* 2000 B.C.

Boy (kouros); probably from Boeotia in Central Greece, marble; *c.* 560 B.C.

of gods who lived on the top of Mount Olympus. Zeus, perhaps better known by his later Roman name, Jupiter, was king or father of the gods. The queen and mother, wife of Zeus, was Hera. The other principal gods, who were regarded as the children of Zeus and Hera, were a brilliant but tumultuous brood, boiling with very human passions and totally unrestrained by the human discipline of conscience.

There were deities in connection with just about every place and event, not to mention physical and mental qualities. There was a goddess of wisdom called Athene, a god of light and thence of enlightenment or knowledge called Apollo; gods of war, of sleep, of social jollity and intoxication; gods of the earth, the sea and the sunless land under the earth where the dead were believed to live; gods of money, metalwork, rivers, springs, mountains and valleys . . . you name it, the Greeks had a god for it.

It is easy to appreciate that in the midst of this profusion of deities, no one ever felt very far away from divine supervision and protection or divine disapproval and vengeance. Such a theology was perhaps somewhat primitive but no more so than naïve forms of Christianity still practised today. Also there is reason to believe that intellectuals like Sophocles, Euripides, Plato and Thucydides reacted sceptically to claims made on behalf of the Homeric deities in much the same way that during the Renaissance educated men began to doubt the literal truth of extensive sections of the Bible. But that did not mean that the most brilliant of the Athenians treated religious ideas lightly and with disrespect.

They were aware, as are the greatest minds of today, of how little we know about all the great metaphysical problems – what we are, why we are, what becomes of us, if anything, when our present existence comes to an end. And we know from the tragedies of Aeschylus, Euripides and Sophocles as well as from the philosophical works of Plato that their scepticism was balanced by the realization of how deeply Athenian institutions and thought were permeated by traditional religious beliefs.

For instance it is one thing for Aeschylus to express in *Prometheus Bound* a highly sceptical, even satirical view of the attitude of Zeus to man as he struggles towards greater mastery of his environment and thence to greater independence of divine authority. It is quite another for even the most intellectual mind to free itself entirely from widely accepted attitudes and beliefs. All Athenians, from the greatest poets and philosophers to the man in the street were intensely aware of being surrounded by intangible but none the less powerful intimations of deity.

The contrast with our own times is immediately apparent. With the Church in decline, our activities in work and play have become to a high degree secularized; divorced from spiritual and instead concentrated on material purposes. For this reason if for none other it ill becomes us to regard Greek culture as a relic of pagan darkness. And yet our attitude is often unbearably smug. Wonderful, we think, that people who lived so long ago should have arrived at such ideas, could have wrought such miracles in stone and metal, and evolved such poetry, music, philosophy and – yes, actually, morals.

Reflecting on the British Museum Greek collection I am bound to wonder what, if any, of our achievements will survive as long. Have there been any really great buildings? Coventry Cathedral, would you say? Or the new Euston Station? Or the United Nations building in New York? Can we claim that Eliot or Auden or Picasso or Benjamin Britten will last like Praxiteles, Phidias or Euripides? We can only guess at the answer. The final verdict does not rest with us but with posterity. But if effort is anything to judge by I would say that our cultural bequest to posterity will be poorer than that of the relatively small city of Athens in the hundred years from 450 to 350 B.C.

We are too concerned with material comforts and the search for leisure with the emphasis not on stimulation but relaxation. We have more than our fair share of vulgarity – in style and taste and achievement. The value of the Greek collec-tion is that it gives us the chance to take an occasional refreshing glance at what is enduring and enriching – not just for you and me and for now, but for life and for ever.

Chapter Six

The Romans

Robert Erskine

Of all the peoples of Antiquity, we have most in common with the Romans. There are, it is true, aspects of their civilization that are abhorrent to us. They accepted slavery in the natural order of things; they relished the horrors of the arena; they exposed unwanted children, and they claimed to be able to foretell future events from the entrails of sacrificed animals. But it was another age, and another intellectual climate. From the Roman standpoint, some of our own habits would seem callous and barbaric; our lack of interest in the aged members of our society for example, and our casual attitude to the duties of friendship.

But it is not the differences between the texture of our society and the Roman, but the similarities that are most striking. They were an energetic people, forth-right and precise. Where Greeks theorized, Romans acted. They would listen to reason, but would quickly become impatient for action. Because they appreciated that circumstances are constantly changing, their laws were left open to interpretation by jurists, and cases were argued on their merits. Their armies were better trained and better organized than any other until modern times. Local government was administered partly by professionals, and partly by elected amateurs, and it worked extremely well. They tolerated the social and religious customs of their provinces, except when it was considered that they endangered the unity of the Empire.

It is still possible to see the influence of the Roman engineers on the shape of the landscape: the aqueducts to carry water into the cities; the harbours; and the famous straight roads. The scale of Roman land-drainage schemes compare favourably with our own; canals were built and rivers were harnessed for transport; and where barbarism threatened the Roman peace, miles of military walls and earthworks straddled the countryside. In the cities, communal works like temples, market-places, baths and theatres take precedence over palaces and private dwellings. The wealthy man was more inclined to construct or restore a public building than to aggrandize his own house. In every-thing Roman there is evidence of a practical disposition, and a strong civic sense.

In its hey-day, the Roman Empire embraced many peoples of completely diverse character, from the Celtic tribesmen of Britain to the sophisticated

1. Antistius Sarculo and his wife Antistia Plutia. Marble commemorative relief erected by two of their freedmen; first century B.C.

Greek townsmen of the Middle East. It is a testimonial to the Imperial policy towards even the most distant provinces that after the initial conquest, most were content to settle down under the Roman organization and to benefit from the security it offered. Conquest was indeed a Roman predilection, whether it was a prophylactic conquest to guarantee lasting safety from hostile neighbours, or whether it was conquest for glory, or for profit. But on the whole, the dominant theme of Roman history is conquest in the pursuit of order. The Romans strove to make their world a well-regulated entity, a world adjusted to the needs of its inhabitants by careful legal sanctions, as well as a world improved by practical efforts to diminish its geographical drawbacks. It was as much an engineer's conquest of nature, as a soldier's conquest of nations.

The Roman energy was self-generating. No god directed their tireless drive. Their sense of purpose grew entirely from the very human conviction that they alone knew best. Yet at all stages in their history they were troubled by political and social problems similar to our own. Civil war was a constant occurrence but it is to their credit that the confrontation was more often to do with principle than with private vainglory.

2. Roman denarii showing portraits of Caesar, Brutus, and Mark Antony

The foundations of this Roman conscientiousness lies in the character of people like Antistius Sarculo, and his wife, Plutia. Here is a pair of formidable elderly people (1), who stare out of their marble block in a completely unself-conscious way. Sarculo is clearly a man used to decision and responsibility: reliable and fair-minded, if a little grim. Nevertheless, there is an attractive quality of self-dignity wrought into the portrait which relieves his severe expression. There was no need to smooth over the lines of age which furrow his features, for he was not ashamed of them. On the contrary, he wears them proudly as a sign of his own individuality. The Romans were proud of themselves, their accomplishments and their integrity. The crisp, factual style of the sculpture proclaims that this couple lived through some of the most stirring times of Roman history, for it is dated between 40 and 30 B.C. They were contemporaries of Julius Caesar, Pompey and Brutus. The inscription states that Sarculo held a priesthood – more of a social or even political appointment than the word suggests today. Roman religion was a religion of the State, rather than of personal conscience. As a public figure, he would have had to support the ancient Republican constitution, or accept the revolutionary rule of a single dictator.

In fact, the dilemmas that he experienced were all too close to those that have troubled us in recent times. There is no record, however, of his political leanings, though we can be sure that he did not shirk his duty.

Roman portrait-sculpture of this period was consistently good, because its intention was to perpetuate an honest vision of the man as he really was, rather than to present him as a stereotype of the man he would like to be. As a tomb-stone, the Sarculo sculpture would have been set up in or outside the family mausoleum, situated by the side of the road leading into the town where he had lived. It was doubly important that the sculpture should express his features with accuracy, so redolent of the austere Roman virtues. Countless people passing by would judge his memory by his portrait, and the evidence of his qualities would survive. It was usual for another head to be kept in the entrance-

3. Sardonyx cameo bust of the Emperor Augustus (27 B.C. to A.D. 14) wearing an aegis;
the gold diadem was added in the Middle Ages

hall of the family house, along with those of other distinguished ancestors of his line. These were paraded in public on the occasion of family events such as marriages and funerals, adding their collective authority to the rites. Here again, tradition contributed to accuracy rather than flattery, for in earlier times it seems that these effigies were of wax, possibly even death-masks. By the first century B.C. the waxwork has given way to more permanent stone, which still retains the literal technique of its prototype.

Through portraits like Sarculo's we can meet the Romans face to face, and feel the presence of the man behind the stone. But we can carry the familiarity even further, and actually hear them talking through the private letters that have come down to us. They are another manifestation of that interest in personality that we have observed in the portraits. Throughout the Roman period, there was a ready market in literary circles for the collected correspon-dence of famous people, because it is in a man's letters that he reveals his character best of all.

The outstanding Roman letter-writer was Marcus Tullius Cicero, the lawyer, who was a contemporary of Sarculo's. His letters to friends were especially valued because they were written in a relaxed, colloquial style in contrast to his more formal essays and legal speeches. In addition, he was himself a great luminary, and he writes to many of the principal figures of his day, or comments on them and the events in which he and his contemporaries are involved. There we can find the most intimate glimpses of the men who were shaping Rome's destiny in political argument and in civil war. They are as fascinating to us as they were to the Romans themselves. He describes with relief the progress of an awkward visit from the dictator Caesar, himself, at the height of his power:

> Caesar proved most affable. When he had arrived at Philippus' house on the evening of 8 December, it was so crowded with soldiers that the room in which he himself was to dine could scarcely be kept clear; two thousand men there were. . . . He wasn't a guest to whom you would say, 'Do please come again on your way back.' Once is enough. Our talk kept off serious topics and was largely about literature. In short, he was delighted and enjoyed himself.

And of Pompey the Great, whose cause he supported, he says sadly:

> He has no graciousness, no straightforwardness, no principles in politics, no glamour or strength or generosity.

But after his ignominious death in Egypt, Cicero relents a little:

> I never had any doubt how Pompey would end. . . . I cannot help being sorry about his fate: in my experience he was an honest, clean and upright man. . . .

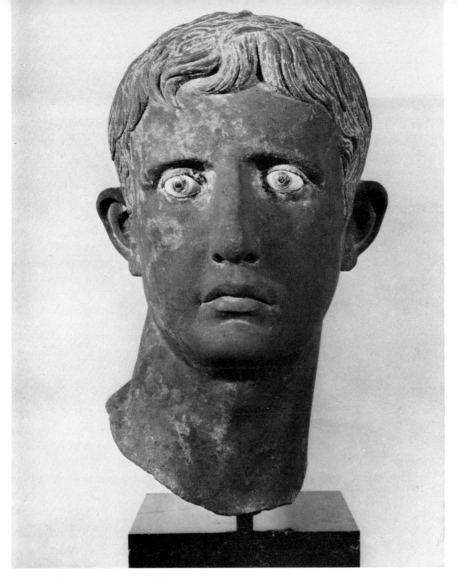

4. Bronze head from a statue of the Emperor Augustus; Roman, first century A.D.

When writing of Brutus, a principal figure in Caesar's murder, he actually quotes the victim's own words:

Caesar used to say, 'It makes no difference what that man wants: but whatever he wants, he wants it passionately.'

And later, in a letter to Brutus himself:

I disagree violently with you, Brutus: I do not admit your doctrine of mercy. . . . You'll be crushed, Brutus, if you don't take care.

His hatred of Mark Antony is evident throughout the correspondence: 'This damned madman' he calls him:

The swashbuckler is out for blood. . . . How could he study anything in a den of vice and drunkenness. . . . No wonder that at times one almost wishes Caesar was still here.

It seems that Cleopatra, the scheming Queen of Egypt, had slighted Cicero somehow: he certainly never forgave her:

I hate the queen. . . . [he says] Her insolence, when she was living in Caesar's house in the gardens beyond the Tiber, I cannot recall without indignation. So no dealings with that lot. They seem to think I have not only no spirit, but no feelings at all.

There are hopeful words about Octavian, the promising young man who Caesar intended as his successor, and who inherited his name:

The boy Caesar has natural strength of character to an extraordinary degree; I only hope that when he is at the height of honour and popularity we may be able to guide and control him as easily as we have been able to control him up to now!

In the event, Cicero turned out to be absolutely wrong. 'The boy Caesar' grew up to be the most ruthless politician of them all: for it was he who gave Mark Antony the opportunity to have Cicero murdered and get this constant critic of tyranny out of the way. Later on, Mark Antony also succumbed to the prevailing fashion for violent death, leaving 'the boy Caesar' high and dry at the summit of power, to become the first Roman Emperor, the Emperor Augustus.

During the Civil Wars the principal contenders wished to advertise their features to the general populace and to their own troops, and the only mass-medium available for propaganda was the coinage. But the Roman denarius (2) was a tiny silver coin, roughly the size of a new penny: here the portraits have to be simplified caricatures, for there was no room for a more detailed treatment. Still, the coins project each personality with great clarity: they enable us immediately to sense the energy and initiative of Caesar; the dogged rectitude

5. Bronze sestertius showing a portrait of the Emperor Nero (*left*)

6. Silver cup with a repoussé decoration showing a scene from a little-known legend; Roman, first century B.C. or A.D. (*opposite above*)

7. A millefiore (glass) bowl from Alexandria (*opposite below*)

of Brutus; and the self-indulgence of the horrible Mark Antony. The old Republican tradition for vivid portraiture continues in these minute profiles, for their aim was to intensify the identity of the people they represented.

How different is the attitude expressed in the splendid cameo-portrait of Augustus! Here (3) is the very personification of autocratic rule that Cicero with his Republican sympathies would have detested. It shows the Emperor in handsome middle-age 'at the height of his honour and popularity'. All of a sudden the honest Roman taste is corrupted by fulsome homage to the ruler. It also represents the new opulence at the Roman capital, for such cameos were precious palace objects: the gifts for other kings and princes. The jewels in the wreath are not original but were added in medieval times.

In private houses, too, frugal tastes give way to ostentation at the dinner-table: it is the period of the finest Roman silverware. The silver cup illustrated here (6) is very much in keeping with the new age of Imperial rule. Virgil is writing his *Aeneid* in the manner of the Homeric poems, just as the relief round the outside of the cup describes a scene from Greek mythology. In Rome, now the centre of the world, the poets and artists celebrate the unfolding of a new Golden Age, in contrast to the horrors of the recent Civil Wars. Augustus is *Pater Patriae* – 'Father of his Country': the paternalistic despot who has gathered the reins of power into his own hands in the name of efficiency and good government.

Meanwhile, in the provinces, the Emperor's statue set up in countless temples emphasizes the Roman presence. Here again, the ancient candour would be quite out of place, for this is art in the service of the State: a propagandist art deliberately designed to impress the provincials with the Emperor's god-like omnipotence. The piercing gaze of the inlaid eyes promises security to the loyal, and retribution to the rebellious. The fine bronze head of Augustus (4) in the British Museum is part of such a statue set up on the very edge of the Roman world at Aswan in Egypt. It was one of hundreds to be found in every corner of the Roman world: indeed making Emperor-statues became a considerable industry. Inevitably, truth suffered at the expense of sensationalism: the statue in the temple was now a symbol of Roman power. Nevertheless, accuracy was still a sculptural virtue, and although the human blemishes have been doctored out, the head is still a reasonable likeness of Augustus. The tradition of literal portraiture in Roman sculpture was so strong, that the Emperor still felt it necessary to summarize his individual *persona*, even in generalized icons such as these.

Throughout the first century A.D., the distinctive features of each emperor are clearly portrayed, not only in the statues but also on the coins. A new coin, the large, bronze sestertius (5), provided a better format for the portrait in relief. The

Emperor Nero, the last of Augustus's dynasty, was content to admit to his bloated appearance. Something of his dangerous character clearly comes across, and it is no surprise that he ended up with a dagger in his overfed body. Nero's death brought civil war once again, and the year A.D. 69 saw the violent demise of no less than three successive emperors. The coinage was always a vital political instrument, for a new emperor could prove his accession to the Roman people so long as his portrait was in circulation. Galba reigned for only nine months, yet coins bearing his head are not uncommon. Otho lasted for three months, and his coins are rarer. The mint never issued any bronze in his name, but his silver denarii exist in considerable quantity. Vitellius managed eight months in power, yet his coins again are quite plentiful today. The quantity of surviving coins struck for these short-lived emperors stresses the importance of this medium of public relations: and, typically, the most powerful factor was the portrait.

The following century and a half is Rome's most prosperous period. Trade flourished across a peaceful Empire, stretching from Britain to Arabia, and from Spain to the Black Sea. Roman goods found their way abroad as well: into the hostile German forests, the Sudanese deserts, and Afghanistan. There were even Roman trading stations in South India. Roman goods are somewhat

8. Red pottery lamp from northern Italy decorated with a head of Jupiter; early second century A.D.

stereotyped, for they had to serve such an extensive market: but even behind these mass-produced wares there lurks that individuality that animates every Roman object. In the first place, there was a variety of choice, because different parts of the Empire specialized in certain classes of goods. The Alexandrian glass-makers produced the elaborate 'millefiore' bowls (7), made of rods of coloured glass all fused together, a difficult process that has never properly been mastered since. In Roman times, they were much admired and were extremely expensive. It was common knowledge that they were Alexandrian products, and they needed no further identification. More commonplace articles often carry the brand-names of the factories that made them, in a spirit of commercial rivalry. The red pottery lamp (8) comes from a North Italian factory, and is stamped 'STROBILI' – (a product) 'of Strobilus', on its base. Bronze pans, better-class pottery, wine-amphorae, and many other goods, bear similar labels. It is possible today to plot the particular trading pattern of a given manufacturer from the examples of his product which crop up in archaeology.

Commercial activity on this scale could only develop in peacetime. The Roman Empire was fringed with enemies kept at bay by the Roman legionaries (9, and cover), excellent soldiers, well trained and loyal to their commanders. There were 6000 legionaries in a Legion, and in the second century there were thirty Legions spread round the perimeter of the Empire. For the most part, their adversaries were barbarians famous for their bravery and enormous numbers. There were defeats, of course. But on the whole such enemies were too much of an unco-ordinated rabble to match the discipline and energy of the Legions. Josephus, the Jewish historian who had seen them in action, recognized the value of their training:

> No panic incapacitates them, no toil wears them out, so that victory over men not so trained follows as a matter of course. It would be not far from the truth to call their drills bloodless battles, their battles, bloody drills.

For all its size, this was no army of anonymous multitudes. A legionary enjoyed many privileges, such as the right to a plot of land after discharge, and the social and legal advantages of Roman citizenship. Even the Emperor might take an interest in the welfare of an individual soldier, as one of Pliny's letters shows:

> Publius Accius Aquila, Sir, a centurion of the sixth cohort in the auxiliary cavalry, has asked me to send you a petition begging your interest in his daughter's citizen status. It was difficult to refuse, especially as I know how readily you give a sympathetic hearing to your soldiers' requests.

Pliny the Younger, another celebrated letter-writer, was made Governor of Bithynia by the Emperor Trajan. Some of the correspondence between the two men is preserved. Here is the reply:

9. Bronze statuette of a Roman legionary; second century A.D.

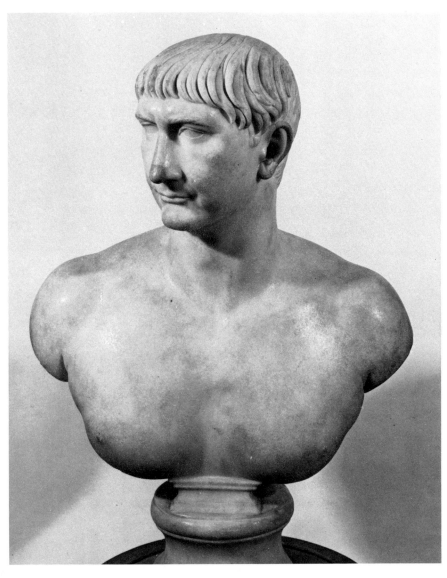

10. A characteristic bust of the Emperor Trajan (A.D. 53–117)

I have read the petition which you forwarded on behalf of Publius Accius Aquila, Centurion of the sixth cohort of cavalry, and have granted his request. I have accordingly given his daughter Roman citizenship and am sending you a copy of the order to hand to him.

Trajan (10) was the greatest of the soldier-Emperors. His people conferred on him the exceptional title of *Optimus Princeps* – 'The best of rulers' – in gratitude for his strong but humane government. In Trajan, the very finest traditions of Rome are personified, even though he came originally from the Spanish provinces. Pliny and his Emperor correspond in 'the honest Roman language of sensible men' (a phrase of Caesar's), and the calm, matter-of-fact tone of the letters demonstrates the extreme professionalism of the Roman Empire at work. The Governor consults the highest authority with all sorts of details of administration:

> Among the chief features of Amastris, Sir (a city which is well built and laid out), is a long street of great beauty. Throughout the length of this, however, there runs what is called a 'stream', but is in fact a filthy sewer, a disgusting eyesore which gives off a noxious stench. The health and appearance alike of the city will benefit if it is covered in, and with your permission this shall be done. . . .

> There is every reason, my dear Pliny, to cover the water which you say flows through the city of Amastris, if it is a danger to health while it remains uncovered. I am sure you will be active as always to ensure that there is no lack of money for this work.

Trajan's portrait confirms what we learn from his own words. Here is a man fully in control of his government: firm but never cruel, intelligent and always active. He would have agreed with Cicero, 150 years before:

> If you ask me, I think a man is finished, when he makes pleasure, not duty, his main object.

Whether we look upon their portraits, or read their letters, the Romans' interest in personality keeps their image alive for us. Even in the most banal commercial goods, Roman objects invariably lead to Roman people. The narrative of Roman history frequently anticipates the events of our own time. We stand in the Roman shadow as we experience again and again the issues that they had to cope with: that is why their arguments, their reactions, and their attitudes provide so clear a perspective for our own understanding.

Chapter Seven

The Romano-British

Gwyn Thomas

The centuries that surround the beginning of the Christian era were a time of convulsion. Tribes moved at random, unhindered by fixed and powerful frontiers. They were impelled by greed for what lay ahead of them and fear of what lay behind them. The primitive methods of production made the accumulation of wealth in any form but loot extremely difficult. Prehistory is a dim map of needs crudely fulfilled, a sniffing of the air and a conscienceless stirring of the tribal body towards better wheat, sweeter water.

Final power would go to him who had the gift of organization, of defining needs and giving the world a physical frame in which most needs could, on a permanent, rational basis, be met. Disciplined, paid armies, capable of understanding and responding to a chain of commands, able not merely to fight wars but to see the furthest objectives of conquest, and to bind their territorial plunder with roads, walls and officials.

The Romans did these things to a Britain for which submission and spoliation were already old familiar traumas. Waves of plunderers, for a good millennium, had been beating on her shores. The rulers the Romans found in Britain were themselves a new graft in this land. Cunobelinus, ruling over most of what we know today as the 'Home Counties', with his sumptuous capital at Colchester (Camulodunum) was a newcomer. Camulodunum. It is strange how many names of this period bring to one's mind the thought of Camelot, the Arthurian vision, after the Roman defeat, of a vanished loveliness and calm, a memory of wealth and goodness despoiled, valour forever vanquished and betrayed.

A relatively new arrival too was Prasutagus, the husband of Boadicea, that termagant of genius, head of the Iceni tribe in East Anglia. They had won their British kingdoms, leading a great influx of settlers into Britain from the European mainland.

The Welsh have a little phrase that throws a strange pathetic light on the successive rapes of this island that culminated finally in the Anglo-Saxon and Norman settlements which gave Britain the beginning of her modern sound and texture. The Welsh, who physically do not resemble the tall, fair Celts described by historians, refer to their own aboriginal ancestors as the '*pobl bach ddu*' – 'the little dark people'. It conjures up perfectly the portrait of a pitifully under-

Bronze shield boss from Wandsworth; *c.* 200 B.C.

developed, ill-equipped and vulnerable tribe, driven to remote valleys, caves, hill-fastnesses, reduced to a primordially bare culture, a fearful evasive existence, a civilization, in short, of hiding.

Welsh mythology is haunted by the image of the cave and magical inter-vention from the spirit world. Their dwellings and fanes, of whatever insub-stantial kind they were, would have been as remote from the capital city of Cunobelinus as Rome was from Colchester.

There was a time when the past drowsed inviolately away. Now it rests uneasily beneath its surface of time, refuse and newly formed top-soils. Deep-delving machines and skilled, patient research are uncovering every day some new aspect of the 400 or 500 years in which the Italian invaders and the con-querors of ill-assorted native tribes took to coalesce into the hyphenated unit of comparatively civilized existence that we call 'Romano-British'.

Our curiosity and knowledge have gone far beyond the giant, indestructible fragments like the walls of Hadrian and Antoninus, meant to intimidate and repel the Picts who came swooping down from the Caledonian hills to take a bite at the soft flesh of Roman towns and villas, or the Roman fort at Cardiff

which provided the place and nucleus of the later Norman castle built seven centuries after the Romans took their leave.

Buried and utterly fascinating fragments of the past have been uncovered in our century. The hill-fort of Segontium at Caernarvon marks one of the spots at which the Legions had perforce to stop at the shores of the Western Sea and stare towards Ireland. Segontium today looks down at Caernarvon Castle, the Normans' greatest and most enduring masterpiece of aggression in the posture of defence. Caernarvon is the perfect summary of the geology of conquest, the way in which conquerors live in a land of dark mountains lit by hating eyes.

And beneath the castles, the walls, the lighthouses, is the soil which awaits the day of respite from the restless needs of men. Into the soil the archaeologists probe ever more brilliantly to discover the private details, the face, the voice, the gestures of the multitudes, now pacific and content, now bewildered and fierce, who lived out their lives through the centuries during which the great emperors and procurators, Caesar, Claudius, Hadrian, Severus, Theodosius, set the iron hand of Imperial power on the tribal ant-hill of pre-Roman Britain.

Coins have been excavated and tabulated, giving us clues to the answering of such massive questions as when the Imperial defence-barriers were dismantled and abandoned. We owe much to man's carelessness and fright. When he is carefree he drops his money about. When he is terrified either by the nightmares of avarice or the sight of plundering hooligans swarming over the nearest hill or the farm walls, he will bury his cash until such time as he can creep back and redeem it. In both cases the historian is grateful. Coins are the fingerprints of sophisticated men. They give us a tangible witness to man's rulers and needs, to what he was willing to put up with politically, and what wolves he was able to keep away from his door economically.

It has been determined that in the villa-sites that have been dug, coins dated before the close of the fourth century have not been found. This settles, at least on the basis of a hopeful approximate, a question that baffled historians for years: when exactly did the nerve and fighting arm of Roman Britain cease to function in the face of the tripartite tide of barbarism, Irish, Scottish, and Saxon, that engulfed and erased all the symptoms of order and graciousness that must have flourished here through the hey-day of Roman power. There must have been a time, the period when the tribes beyond the *limites*, the boundaries, the walls, were silenced and still and the ruling groups of the native tribes spoke Latin and

Flagon, bluish-green glass; Barnwell, Cambridgeshire; late first century

planted in Britain the political pattern of the Roman municipality, when life had something approaching serenity, a purpose, an acceptable point, a seemingly enchanted interlude in man's baffled fight against the pestilential and unbearable, a creative integration of the Roman invader with the people who were here before him.

Alongside the cash of the market and the pocket, there is the currency of the spirit, man's effort to match life's more inscrutable elements with his own capacity for sustained and elaborate prayer. Ever since its erection, Britons have known that the Romans had a goddess called Minerva and that they built a grand and lovely temple to her at Bath. Centuries later, we found at Lydney a temple to Nodens, the hunter, god of the Forest of Dean, a deduction made from the frequency of the hound motif in its decoration.

The abundance of coins found there suggested that the temple must have been a place of busy pilgrimage. And the layout of the walls indicate that by the time of its establishment in the fourth century the architectural ideas of the Roman pagan temple-builders were edging towards the pattern we now identify with the

Electrum torc from the Snettisham treasure; first century B.C. (*left*)

Bronze mirror back from Desborough, Northamptonshire; an example of Late Celtic art first century A.D. (*right*)

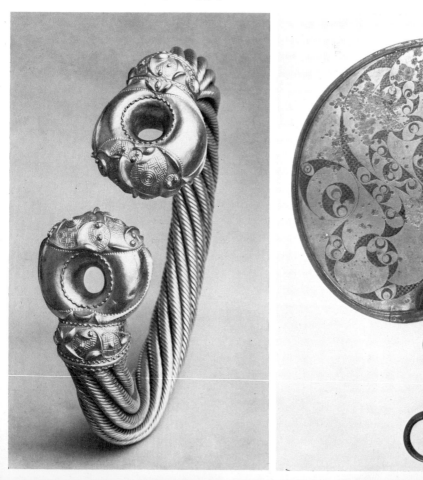

Castor-ware beaker
with barbotine hunting
scene; second to
mid-fifth century

Christian chapel. This recession of a vigorous belief in the pantheon that had
sustained Republican Rome and which had been debased and enfeebled by
emperor-worship is of the highest significance. One of the first buildings of
truly Roman magnificence comparable with anything to be found in the seat
and heart of the Empire was the temple raised at Colchester and dedicated to the
god-monarch Claudius. One of the last monuments of the Romano-British
Age is that temple at Lydney, modest and already touched by the much more
intensely personal ethos of the Christians.

When men find that they no longer have a robust confidence in their traditional
gods they are ready for a great step forward or backward. In the case of the
Romans in Britain, in the fourth and fifth centuries A.D., the step they were to
take was backwards, into the dark and forever. And there are pages of enchant-
ment that have been revealed by pure chance. In Chedworth in the Cotswolds
a landowner lost a ferret of which he was besottedly fond. The animal had
disappeared into a pile of ancient and undeciphered rubble. The landowner
peered into the dark recesses of the mound. Inside he saw gleams of coloured
light. Two gleams were the green eyes of the trapped ferret. The others were the
first glimpses modern man had had of a magnificent tessellated Roman pave-
ment, part, in an older time, of a luxurious villa. It had among its other appurten-
ances a *fullonica*, a fuller's shop, which testified to the extension of the textile trade
in the period of its power and the ascendancy of the wool trade in the Cotswold
hills. Reminding us of Dr Glyn Daniel's discovery, when still a very young
archaeologist, of a Roman mosaic floor beneath the dull, undistinguished
premises of a bakehouse in his native village of Llantwit Major in South Wales.

The story of the Romano-British experience is one of simple, dramatic force:

Bronze head of Hadrian from the Thames at London Bridge; second century A.D.

the classic pattern of violence, pain, conciliation, enfeeblement and death. Dolts and geniuses, saints and villains bow briefly into the light, deposit their customary loads of good and evil, then vanish. In the light of the centuries that stand between us and them, the period of fulfilment and decline is relatively brief and in most respects now, with the scholars' help, beautifully clear.

It has something of the vibrant urgency of that other quickly lived and easily remembered saga of strange men, in strange places, facing brave and relentless enemies, the opening of the American West. With the difference that our equivalent of the Red Indians, the Britons, lost not once but twice. They went down to the Romans and to the barbarians who came over the seas and walls to destroy the Imperial eagles and the domesticated doves of the pacified provinces. Also, the white man in America remained the master. The Romans lived in a time when races and tribes were more mobile, more easily replaceable.

And again, the ground on which the Romano-British saga was played out is the ground we walk on. Eboracum, the Roman town and fortress from which the invaders organized their second thrust towards the north, is now York. Devum and Isca, the stations that kept a stern eye on the tribes of the south-

Display shield, bronze with glass,
found in the Thames near Battersea;
Late Celtic art; first century B.C.
to first A.D.

Harness trappings from
the Stanwick hoard, Yorks;
Early Celtic; first century A.D.

west, the Dubonni and Silures, are now Gloucester and Caerleon. Virconium, in north-west England, was the fourth largest city in Roman Britain and the central muscle in the Roman campaigns to subdue the tribes of the north-Welsh hills, the Deceangli and Ordovices. It is now Wroxeter.

Some of these places have diminished drastically in size and importance, others have mightily waxed. The chemistry of social, economic and military imperatives is not always scrutable. In 1939, the foundations of Claudius's vast temple at Colchester were incorporated into the town's Air Raid Precautions Scheme. There are parts of Britain where the Romans have been missed, that could have done with the preservation of a few implacable tribes of aborigines to serve as a target of attention from the developers of communications and industry.

Having been the stage for this great play, and it is arguable that no phase in the rise and fall of the Roman Empire, 'ordinary men doing extraordinary things', has greater continuous interest than the arrival and departure of the Legions. Through the gaps in the fabric of reconstruction created by the historians and detectives blows the astonishing wind of folk-memory. Tribal recollection is a sensitive and very retentive thing. Disasters make up most of the stitches in a national experience and they are the things that come most readily to the finger-tips as we feel back into our past. Things whispered round tribal fires at night often have as great a validity as any votive-tablet found in a cellar of Hadrian's Wall or a Roman villa at Lullingstone in Kent.

My father was no scholar but a man who kept an attentive and imaginative ear to the groundswell of folk-gossip and racial nostalgia, the neurotic illusion or conviction that we once cut a better figure in the world than we do now. It is as current in the streets of contemporary Rome as it is among the hills of Glamorgan, where before the end of the first century A.D. the Silurian people looked up at the Roman forts that dominated every strategic hill and river confluence and gave up the ghost.

My father was proud of the Silurians and the long ferocity with which they had confronted the standards of the Legions. He was as proud of them as he was of the budgets of Lloyd George which he saw as striking a blow of vindication for the dead Deceangli and Ordovices of North Wales, who frightened the wits out of Suetonius's men on the Island of Mona which we call Anglesey.

He and I stood one day on a high rock overlooking the Vale of Glamorgan, and Silurian murmurs and the barked commands of Vespasian, the gifted rough-neck who laid the first whip on the British west and rose to wear the Imperial Purple in Rome, were strong on the wind. My father pointed to a field a half-mile away and said, out of the dreaming blue, 'It was there, along the banks of that stream that our prince, the Silurian hero, Ely, was routed by

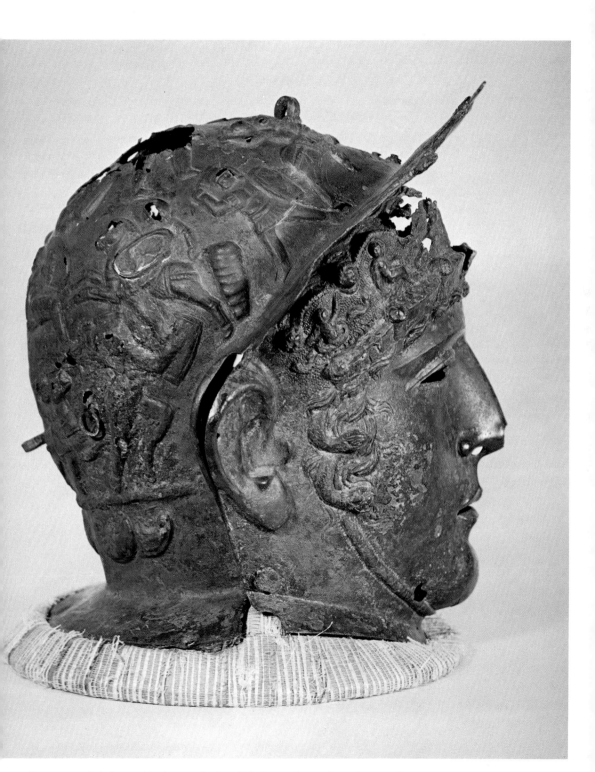

Bronze parade helmet with visor mask, from Ribchester, Lancashire; first or early
second century A.D.

the Second Augustan Legion.' So do the ghosts, without let, hindrance, pass-
port or increased fares, move through the broadest tracts of time.

The beginning of the Roman Conquest strikes a note of mystery. Julius
Caesar came in 55 B.C. and returned the next year. He drubbed Cassivellaunus,
head of the Belgic tribes, then holding the English south-east. When he left
in 54 B.C. he did not come back. He had found the fuel he needed for his drive
against Pompey and towards the Imperial Crown. Rome did not return to
Britain until A.D. 43. The gap in time is long and has puzzled historians.
During these years Rome passed from Republic to Empire. The extension of
territories had created in Rome men of extraordinary wealth. Men with much
money are driven by an inescapable urge to make it more. The minerals and
grain of Britain with the labour force to go along with them were tempting. They
were taken. The Britons showed resentment, courage, fury, but to no avail.

The poetic fury of the Celtic charioteers ran into men who fought by the year,
not the hour, who could stand still under danger as implacably as they moved
forward. Men who fight for pay, commanded by men who plan for power and
profit are rarely resistible. The centurions were the spine of Roman strength;
the financiers and usurers who came to high noon in the Rome of Augustus and
Julius were the brain. They won the world.

In the first wave of the Claudian invasion of A.D. 43 there was a violent spasm
of resistance led by Caractacus, son of Cunobelinus. He lives on in Welsh
legend as Caradoc. He rallied the tribes of the south-east, the Trinovantes, the
Cantiaci, the Regnenses. They broke. The Silures of South Wales and the
Dubonni of the west Midlands accepted him as their leader. They fought and
fled. His last stand, this time leading a host from north-west Wales, was at a
place presumed to be at or near the Long Mynd in Shropshire at a spot still
called 'Caer Caradoc' – 'Caradoc's fort'. He was taken captive to Rome and
his words spoken as he was taken by his guards to admire the splendours of
Rome still provide an oil of pride for the lamp of Celtic myth. 'Why should you
who have so much have fallen upon us who have so little?'

In Trinity House Square in London the tombstone of Julius Classicianus
was discovered. He was Procurator of Britain from A.D. 61 to 65. His predecessor, Suetonius Paulinus, had taken the Legions to North Wales and
launched them across the Menai Straits to massacre the embattled Druids who
were the nearest our aboriginal ancestors ever came to having a political leadership. They had to be destroyed and Suetonius, a thorough and splenetic man,
saw that they were.

The robed Bards who stand round the gorsedd circle at the Welsh National
Eisteddfod are a pathetic attempt to revive a national mood and personality cut
to bits by the Romano-British centuries ago. Not long ago a contractor preparing

a site for one of the new Anglesey industries uncovered a chain. He put it to use. It was a slave-chain that had been used by the Druids for use on victims of the ceremonies of human sacrifice to which the Druids were prone in moments when they thought the holy mistletoe an insufficiently potent totem.

While Suetonius was wiping out resistance in the north-west, the south-east was coming to the boil. The initial shock of defeat and the years of timid conciliation were over. Camulodunum (Colchester), settled by veterans of the new multi-national Roman army, had been founded as the new capital, with the Temple of Claudius the god as its heart. What students of racketeering in the modern world would call the 'enforcers' went busily around stripping the local princelings and chiefs of their privileges and treasure.

One of the chieftains thus despoiled was Prasutagus, of the Iceni, in East Anglia. His queen, Boadicea, was violated and dispossessed along with her daughters. She, like Caractacus, still rides around the Welsh memory, her streaming hair, crazed eyes, and scythed chariot-wheels the symbols of the futile wrath of those doomed by their own inadequacy to be driven out of history. She burned and sacked the rich Roman settlements. Colchester and London were put to the torch. Archaeologists have traced the ash-line of destruction and fondled the skulls of those who were slain and flung into burial-pits by the cartload. The skulls are of the round Mediterranean type, not the long-headed sort in which Boadicea and her avenging multitudes had their last, horrendous thoughts. Bones like those of the defenders overborne in Vespasian's assault on Maiden Castle in Dorset, reveal more in death than in life.

Suetonius hurried south. This time there was no Caractacus to slip away and fight again and kindle the dream of a united front of Celts against the terrible fact of an army backed by a civil service and a strong, central government. Suetonius took a terrible revenge. Nero, a shrewder man than fiction would have us believe, was advised that Suetonius's reprisals would either eliminate or eternally offend the natives; he recalled Suetonius and replaced him with Julius Classicianus.

The new Procurator was a milder, craftier man. He eased the tension. The bloodied rabble of insurgents ebbed back to their villages. Classicianus had a memorial stone raised to him in Trinity House Square. That is appropriate. It is a name associated with a sensible provision of light for benighted voyagers. Nero, who traditionally burned Rome, helped at least to limit the range of arson in this island of Britain.

After that, Romanization swept on methodically. The great roads divided the land into sections, inside which the British population could be supervised, policed, taxed and encouraged to make their compact with the conqueror ever more secure and fertile. Between the years A.D. 78 to 85 Agricola subdued northern England and brought the Caledonians to heel at the Battle of Mons Graupius. Between 122 and 133 Hadrian sealed Scotland off with the great fortified barrier from Tyne to Solway. We can still look at, touch, the amphorae from which freezing legionaries, recruited from the hot lands of Italy, Spain, Scythia, poured their wine, and the bowls from which they spooned their gruel as they looked north at the Scottish Highlands. We can admire the mirrors and trinkets with which they consoled their wives for their long absences.

The disintegration of Roman Britain can be followed in terms of the failure and decay of the whole Roman Imperial system. Thrones begat demented competitors for their occupation. One of the hinges of our own Romano-British destiny can be found in the activities of Clodius Albinus in the years A.D. 196–7. The arms of the octopus had begun to covet the rotten centre. Albinus, Governor of Britain, drained the British garrison to furnish an army to fight for the Roman throne. He was defeated and killed in southern Gaul by the grimly gifted and inexorable African and future emperor, Severus. Hadrian's Wall was overrun and partially destroyed by the barbarian tide which was building up all around the Romanized areas of Britain.

The last two centuries of the Romano-British Age were times of anguished contractions and desperate returns. In A.D. 410, the Emperor Honorius advised the municipalities of Britain to look to their own defences. That was the end. In A.D. 433 according to the Welsh monk Gildas, the Britons sent a heart-broken cry for help to the Roman General Aetius. 'The wild men from without drive us to the sea. The sea drives us back to the wild men from without. We have but one choice. To die with the taste of salt or blood upon our lips.'

At what kind of life could those Britons look back who saw their world crumble before the assaults of the Picts, Scots and Anglo-Saxons. The legends that have gathered round the name of their last leader, Arthur, suggested that they looked back from a present of appalling sorrows to a past that had a golden light, ample in its sustenance, sweet and clement in its mood. Legends apart, it is hard to doubt that Britain in the highest and best years of Romano-British co-existence, was a place infinitely preferable to the Britain found by Aulus Plantius in A.D. 41.

There would have been, of course, the unassimilable fringes, furtively hostile, the *pobl bach ddu*, the cowering, self-alienating elements who could never adjust to the basically alien framework of remorselessly disciplined and exacting routine. But for those who accepted the new standards the rewards were high. Researches into the towns and villas of Roman Britain, Silchester and Lulling-stone outstanding among them, have shown that in terms of amenity, order and civic expression they set levels that the average town of today could not afford or achieve.

Silver bowl and lid from the Mildenhall treasure, Suffolk; fourth century A.D.

The spaces given over to the basilicas and forums, the town halls and public squares, and the lavish provision for municipal bath-houses meant that the people were extremely secure, sociable, articulate and clean. And those attributes are the beginnings of a true and admirable civilization.

Things beget their opposites. At the heart of perversity is a deep, ingenious patience. The Romanizing visitors, Classicianus and the wise Hadrian, gave voice. And out of the mist a twisted echo announces the coming of Hengist and Horsa, invited here by one of the Celts the Legions had subdued 400 years before. It was the end of a rich and peculiar interlude in the British story.

Chapter Eight

Medieval and Later Antiquities

Antonia Fraser

Like Horace Walpole, I have always derived a vigorous pleasure from the historical associations of beautiful objects. In the Department of Medieval and Later Antiquities its rather stern title conceals a rare treasure-house for those who feel that the haze of history shimmering round a priceless hoard is an additional halo enhancing it. I can well understand how Walpole in the eighteenth century amused himself with passion in the collection of such relics – something as he once put it with 'the true rust of the Barons' Wars'. For me the most exquisite object is still in some way still further glorified by an additional association with a particular character or perhaps incident from the past.

The feeling originates with one of wonder at the survival of these antiquities, many of which have indeed been the objects of some sort of miraculous preservation. They are, in the words of Francis Bacon, 'the remnants of history which have casually escaped the shipwreck of time'. Then there is ordinary human curiosity – was this the size of Mary Queen of Scots' finger as revealed by her finger-ring? – leading on to the more elevated historical curiosity – what does the ring tell us about her political attitudes? One should never forget that the people who owned these objects were once alive like us, and that like us they gave presents, wore rings, collected souvenirs, played the guitar, fell in love, went to war and had their horoscopes cast. 'Dryasdust' history – to borrow Carlyle's phrase of opprobrium for anything he did not agree with – is not only distressing to digest, but it is also hardly true history, because these personages, whatever their passions, intrigues, faults and virtues, were certainly not 'dryasdust' when they were living out their dramatic life-stories.

But to proceed further – on a strict historical level of proper information, a Department of the scope and variety of Medieval and Later Antiquities is like a collection of visual documents, in some cases merely illustrating what we know happened, but in others acting as guides to show us for the first time the exact course of events. The Department's multifarious prizes include the pre-eminent Sutton Hoo find (1), the greatest post-Roman excavation in British history, as well as Renaissance jewels, bronze medals, a variety of personal relics from Robert Burns's punch-bowl to Lord Palmerston's Garter, a mass of porcelain and much early Wedgwood. There is also a splendidly cacophonous

1. The gold buckle from
the Sutton Hoo find

room crowded with clocks and watches whose carillons give melodious (if sometimes slightly contradictory) warnings of the hour to the passing visitor. 'Fly envious Time till thou run out thy race' – it is perhaps into this tuneful chamber that Milton's envious Time has honourably retired.

The Strasbourg clock (2), more than five feet high, catches one's eye. Made by Isaac Habrecht in 1589 for Pope Sixtus V, it was a copy of a great astronomical clock in Strasbourg Cathedral – a lofty symbol of the princely commissions of the Renaissance. Another princely commission near by, the large golden *Nef* or Ship Clock (3), probably made for the Emperor Rudolf II in 1581 by Hans Schlottheim of Augsburg, stands for the majestic prestige of the Holy Roman Emperor in sixteenth-century Europe. A *Nef* or ornamental boat had been used to mark the position of royalty at table since medieval times, but Rudolf's *Nef*, with its intricate clockwork elaborated the concept. As Emperor, Rudolf acquired his power formally from the votes of the College of Electors who nonetheless owed allegiance to him. Among the variety of moving figures on the Ship Clock there are to be seen the small golden effigies of the Electors. As they bow their heads in submission to the Emperor, he in return graciously nods his head and waves the hand that contains the sceptre. One can well appreciate how the Emperor Rudolf must have enjoyed having this particular

2. The Strasbourg clock,
made by Isaac Habrecht, 1589

princely commission trundled along his dinner-table on its wheeled carriage.

Less subservient to the Emperor, it seems, was the attitude of John Dee, the famous scientist-cum-astrologer of the period. Dee lectured him so interminably on alchemy that the Emperor finally turned wearily away. But the strange objects which together constitute John Dee's magic apparatus are among the most interesting relics in the Department's collection. There are wax discs (4 and 5), inscribed with mystic names and figures, for placing on his magic table or beneath its legs, an engraved gold disc (6) that Dr Dee is believed to have owned for a while, and finally the obsidian Aztec mirror, probably brought to Europe from Mexico by a Spanish courtier (7). This dark, highly polished object, known either as 'John Dee's Magic Speculum', or the 'Devil's Looking-Glass', was used to communicate with the spirits of the dead. John Dee, an extraordinary individual whose intellectual energies certainly qualify him for the traditional all-round denomination of 'the Renaissance man', is best known as Astrologer to Queen Elizabeth I. He cast his first horoscope for her when she was a young Princess, but got into trouble for casting that of her sister Queen Mary Tudor at the same time. This venture into the royal future amounted to treason by the standards of the time, especially as Mary's prognosis was not particularly

3. The Nef, or Ship, clock, made for the Emperor Rudolf II *c.* 1580; attributed to
Hans Schlottheim of Augsburg

4 and 5. Two of Dr John Dee's wax discs

favourable. Later when Elizabeth's fortunes soared (as Dee had duly predicted) it was Dee who was entrusted with the responsibility of calculating the most auspicious day for her coronation. Queen and scientist continued to enjoy a mutual interest in such studies. On a visit to Dee's Mortlake home in 1575 Elizabeth demanded not only to be shown one of his famous 'glasses' but also to have its properties demonstrated – 'which I did' John Dee himself tells us 'to her Majestie's great contentment and delight'.

Clearly the whole episode was courtly and fit for the scientific sensibilities of a Queen. But Dee's seers, or mediums, on whom he relied to relay him the news from the world of the spirits, were not always so gently mannered – or as honest as Dee himself. Edward Kelley, his most publicized seer, was later satirized as a fraud in Samuel Butler's *Hudibras*:

> Kelly did all his Feats upon
> The Devil's Looking-Glass, a stone
> Where playing with him at Bo-Peep
> He solv'd all problems ne'er so deep.

As Kelley once had the temerity to pass on a message from the spirits instructing Dee to exchange wives with him (it was perhaps not a coincidence that Mrs Dee was more attractive than Mrs Kelley) one can appreciate the sting of Butler's wit. Yet leaving aside Kelley's antics, the history of Dee's magic mirror is so strange that one is almost inclined to credit the mysterious object with the superstitious value it originally held in the sixteenth century.

Some of Dee's possessions were bought by the great antiquary Sir Robert Cotton and on his death they passed with the rest of Cotton's collection to the

British Museum. But the magic mirror mysteriously disappeared. It was the enthusiast Horace Walpole a century later who recognized it as he was rum/maging among the belongings of Lord Frederick Campbell, son of the Duke of Argyll. Walpole himself tells the story of how Lord Frederick inquired casually what on earth the peculiar oval could possibly be. 'I screamed out: "Oh Lord, I am the only man in England that can tell you: it is Dr Dee's black stone!"' The mirror now came temporarily to rest as Walpole's talisman – for he attributed to its magic powers the fact that a burglar who ransacked his house and belongings in his absence, nevertheless failed to steal a single object. Surely it was the stone which protected his collection. And it is Walpole's handwriting which can be seen on the mirror's eighteenth/century case, record/ing its history, with Samuel Butler's satirical verse inscribed in another hand/writing, just beneath it.

After Walpole's death and the great Strawberry Hill sale of his belongings the mirror once more vanished into obscurity. It was last heard of at an auction in 1892 and was generally believed to have ended up at Dresden, where almost certainly it would have been destroyed in the wartime bombing. But in 1966, Mr Hugh Tait, now Acting Keeper of the Department, was told that a bishop was in his waiting/room, bearing with him the Devil's Looking/Glass of John

6. Gold disc, at one time probably in the possession of John Dee (*left*)

7. John Dee's Magic Speculum, or 'Devil's Looking/Glass' (*right*)

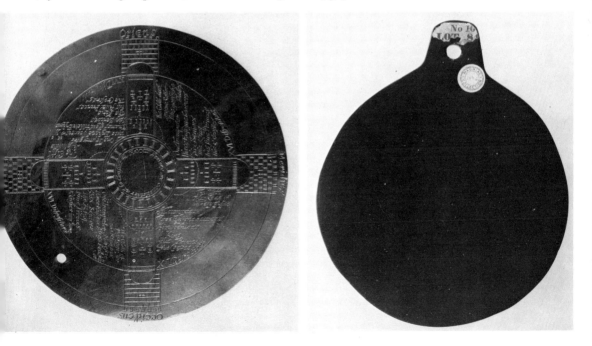

Dee! Mr Tait, with Walpole's expertise and also his enthusiasm, instantly recognized the mirror for what it was – the long-lost instrument of Dee's magic. So the mirror has come to join the other pieces of Dr Dee's apparatus, and now safely confined to its showcase, is exhibited with an authentic provenance from the date of Dee's death.

Two signet-rings in the collection of the Department's personal relics have romantic as well as historical associations. The personal signet ring of King Richard I (8) is marked *Reg. P* for *Regis Privatum* indicating that it was used for private letters rather than official documents. The lettering has been deliberately defaced with blows, as was customary on the death of a sovereign, to prevent his seal being employed subsequently for forgeries. But it is possible that in place of the antique dark green jewel (which is slightly loose) a large ruby was once set in the gold. In this case the ring might well be the famous signet-ring of King Richard, part of the legend of his capture in hostile Germany on his way back from a pilgrimage to the Holy Land. It was a story which obsessed me as a child, as part of the Cœur de Lion myth. There are two versions, both featuring the ring. In one story Richard, dressed as a servant to avoid recognition, was turning the spit in the great hall of the castle where he was spending the night when the magnificent ring gleaming on his finger (which no menial could have possessed) drew attention to his disguise. In the other version King Richard is supposed to have sent his signet-ring to the local lord of the castle asking for a safe passage through his domains, but giving his name merely as Hugo, a merchant. But the local lord, reading the lettering on the ring, and realizing that this was no humble pilgrim but the King of England himself, had him arrested and imprisoned – an imprisonment which only ended, as I fondly believed, with Richard's romantic rescue through the help of his faithful minstrel Blondel.

The second signet ring (9) belonged to Mary Queen of Scots. When writing her biography, the colophon on the underside of the ring (10) seemed so appropriate to her character and aims that I had it used on the cover of the book as an emblem. The seal itself shows the royal lion of Scotland, but the emblem beneath is one of those meaningful monograms Mary loved to employ in writing and embroidery. It consists of the Greek letters M and Phi interwoven – representing Mary and Francis, her first husband, the King of France, who died when she was only eighteen. The interest of this monogram lies in the fact that experts now believe from the general feel of the ring that it must have been made in Scotland after Mary's return, rather than in France. It therefore demonstrates how Mary clung to memories of her French alliance. Not only that, but we find the same emblem in the embroideries executed during Mary's captivity in England many years later. In the tapestries preserved at Oxburgh Hall, Norfolk, the M and Phi symbol can be detected in the corner of at least four of them: yet

8. King Richard I's personal signet-ring; gold set with antique gem engraved with the figure of Minerva

these embroideries were carried out fifteen years after Francis's death, and Mary had been married in the interval to both Darnley and Bothwell. I like to think that the use of the monogram symbolized the continuing importance of Mary's French childhood and marriage in her mind – memories of happiness and security, perhaps, in a life not overburdened with such enjoyments.

A greater contrast could hardly be imagined between Mary's historic but comparatively primitive ring and the intricate splendour of the Lyte Jewel (11). Part of the Waddesdon Bequest, it is one of the many exquisite examples of Renaissance jewellery in the Department. Their existence has always seemed to me to constitute a powerful argument for living at the turn of the sixteenth and seventeenth centuries when, as the portraits show, such luxurious ornaments were proudly worn. But the beauty of the Lyte Jewel is further enhanced by the fact that it represents two arts in one. The exterior is richly enamelled in the most brilliant yet delicate colours, and set with diamonds – but the miniature of King James I within was painted by Nicholas Hilliard. The Lyte Jewel was not in fact a present for a lady: it was granted by King James to Thomas Lyte of Somerset, and the R visible on the outside – an amalgamation of I and R – stands for *Iacobus Rex*. Lyte's acquisition of the jewel shows up one early obsession of the Stuart monarchy in England – their need to prove themselves as a British, rather than a strictly Scottish family. Lyte was an antiquarian and a genealogist: he drew up of his own accord 'a most royally ennobled' family tree for James I, illustrated as Camden described it, with 'admirable flourishes of painting'. The chart was duly presented, the King studied it, and finding that he was happily traced back to 'Brute, the most noble founder of the Britons' rewarded the genealogical speculation handsomely with the present of the Lyte Jewel.

Elizabeth I, James's immediate predecessor, certainly shared the contemporary passion for jewels, many of which are commemorated in her hieratic portraits. But the gittern, or early guitar, in the Department, which is engraved jointly with her arms and those of Robert Dudley, Earl of Leicester, evokes more poignantly than a jewel the greatest of Elizabeth's romances. The gittern itself,

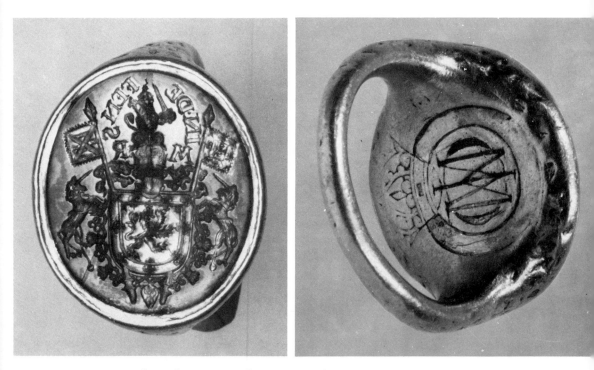

9 and 10. The finger-ring of Mary Queen of Scots

with its elaborate carvings of animals, huntsmen and foliage, dates from the thirteenth century, but in 1578 it was restored, and the two coats of arms engraved on the new silver covering given to the pegbox. Although we do not know which of the two, Elizabeth or Leicester, was responsible for the restoration, the refurbished instrument must surely stand for some delightful joint musical enterprise between the Queen and the courtier, who, in a contemporary phrase 'saw further into her mind than any man'. Yet the date 1578 has an ominous connotation: it was the year of Leicester's secret marriage to the sultry Lady Essex, after twenty years of devotion to Elizabeth, devotion which for reasons of State Elizabeth would never reward with matrimony. Although Elizabeth did not learn of the ceremony till the next year, when the news of the open Court secret did come to her ears, her rage and hurt was so extreme that the old intimacy with Leicester was shattered. In time she did receive Leicester back at Court – although never his wife – but one fancies there were few joint musical enterprises thereafter.

As a character Leicester has glamour, but it is glamour cast by the glittering shadow of Elizabeth's love, falling across his personality and illuminating it beyond its merits. The attraction of my seventeenth-century hero Prince Rupert of the Rhine is original and all his own. The unique stoneware bust of the Prince

(13) produced by John Dwight of Fulham in about 1670, does more for me to convey his powerful allure than, for example, the contemporary portraits by Lely and Honthorst. It is in fact modelled, if not too closely, on an engraving taken from a Lely portrait, but the unknown sculptor must certainly have been a master of his art. The experimental technique used by Dwight at his Fulham pottery in having his material sculpted rather than directly cast, formed part of his unsuccessful attempts to discover the secret of porcelain: thus the bust occupies an important place in its own right in the history of English ceramics. It certainly seems peculiarly appropriate that Prince Rupert should be commemorated by a work of art which was of itself something in the nature of an experiment. By the 1670s Rupert was a man of fifty, no longer the young and dashing cavalier and cavalry hero of the Civil War; at this period of his life he was turning his rapidly inventive mind to scientific innovations, ranging from the improvement of gunpowder to the art of the mezzotint, which, although he did not initiate it, he demonstrated to the diarist John Evelyn with his own hands. One likes to think that a striking likeness was achieved by the bold lines of the ceramic sculpture. We know from Pepys that in his late forties, a few years before this bust would have been conceived, Prince Rupert was still considered one of the best tennis-players in England. The bold lines of this bust seem to reveal something of Rupert's inherited Stuart charm, and also the demonic energy which was all his own.

The other bust in the Department which exercises a peculiar fascination is the exotic early thirteenth-century golden 'head reliquary' of St Eustace, from the Cathedral at Basle (14). Here it is the astonishing almost barbaric splendour of the head which attracts one, rather than any historic significance; and yet the reliquary does have a history of some macabre interest beyond mere magnificence of appearance. When it was originally acquired by the Museum in the middle of the last century, it was assumed that the golden head contained the relics of the Saint stored within it. But about fifteen years ago, when the golden head was dismantled for cleaning, a second identical plain wooden head was found inside it. The lid of the wooden head then lifted off to reveal the relics of St Eustace and other saints carefully preserved inside in thirteenth-century cotton-wool. The relics were dispatched back to the Cathedral, but the wooden head (and incidentally the cotton-wool) is carefully preserved in the Department. So finely is it carved, that it was probably originally intended to stand on its own, before some access of affluence led to its enrichment. It now stands side by side with the golden head, looking rather like some poverty-stricken *doppel-gänger*, come back to haunt his rich relation.

Lastly, I am attracted to two remarkable examples of Francis Bacon's theory of antiquities as casual survivors of time's shipwreck. The Royal Gold Cup (15), is one of the great treasures of the Department, and indeed of the Museum. To go further one might aptly describe it as a national treasure since it was classed as such among the Crown Jewels in the reign of Henry VIII and Elizabeth I. But its history has at all points been quite as dramatic as its glorious heraldic appearance. Made of solid gold, and weighing altogether over four pounds, it is ornamented with scenes from the life of St Agnes. It was probably made in France in the late fourteenth century as a present for King Charles V, who being born on the Feast of St Agnes (21 January) had a particular devotion to the Saint. On the death of Charles's son, Charles VI, the cup seems to have been bought by the Regent of England, the Duke of Bedford, and on his death the cup passed to his nephew, the young King Henry VI. It was among the jewels pawned from the Royal Collection to pay for the invasion of Normandy.

Little more was heard of the cup until 1883 when the Abbess of a Spanish convent near Burgos put it up for sale. No one had any idea how the convent came into possession of it and it was sent to Paris for inspection by a noted collector Baron Pichon. He deciphered the Latin inscription added later to the stem of the cup: 'This cup of solid gold, a relic of the royal treasure of England, and a memorial of the peace made between the Kings, the Constable Juan de Velasco, returning thence after successfully accomplishing his mission, presented as an offering to Christ the Peacemaker.' It was established that the inscription referred back to the peace concluded between James I and Philip III of Spain in 1604, when the chief of the Spanish mission had indeed been Juan de Velasco, Duke of Frias. Unfortunately, in tracing the cup's history, Baron Pichon became involved in a lawsuit with the descendant of the Duke of Frias, who considered that the cup had been presented to the convent in 1610 on terms which precluded its resale. However, in the end the Duke lost his case and the cup remained in Paris till the end of the last century, when it happily came the way of the museum. First a French treasure, then part of the interwoven history of England and France, then the symbol of an Anglo-Spanish peace, it now stands unique among what were once a mass of great English royal treasures – having survived financial disaster, revolution, war and obscurity.

The story of the Lewis Chessmen (12) is less royally emblazoned, but equally to be marvelled at. The chessmen date from the twelfth century, and are either English or Scandinavian in origin, but they were discovered completely by accident on the coast of the remote Scottish Island of Lewis, part of the Outer Hebrides. An exceptional spring tide carried away part of the coastline in 1831, and a small subterranean building, looking rather like an oven, was uncovered from a sandbank. A local inhabitant decided to investigate the 'oven' with his spade, but the sight which greeted him – nearly a hundred grave small white figures distributed about the interior – so unnerved him that he decided he was

11. The Lyte Jewel, English, early seventeenth century

12. The Lewis Chessmen; Scandinavian;
found on the Isle of Lewis (Outer Hebrides) in 1831;
made of morse ivory and sperm-whale ivory (*below*)

13. Prince Rupert; stoneware bust by John Dwight; *c.* 1680

interrupting an assembly of elves and fairies, flung down his spade and fled. But his wife who had a stronger nerve made him return and thus the chessmen – a total of seventy-eight chessmen and fourteen draughtsmen – were rediscovered. Because the cache forms part of several sets, rather than one complete set, it is believed that these chessmen were in fact part of the stock of a travelling salesman.

Even a personal connection as far away and unexpected as a seafaring mer-chant 800 years ago, who dealt among other goods in Romanesque chessmen and was shipwrecked on a lonely Scottish shore in the course of his rounds, seems to enhance the curious offbeat appeal of the chessmen and bring them more closely into the texture of our historical imagination. The double life of such relics is epitomized by the great Sword of State in the Department which was once carried before the child Edward V, as Prince of Wales. On the one hand it symbolizes the power and authority of the monarchy in fifteenth-century England, such swords of State having being employed to mark the royal dominion since the coronation of Ethelred in 978. On the other hand we remember the mysterious disappearance of the young King, with his brother the Duke of the York, within the confines of the Tower of London, and we

15. The Royal Gold Cup; French; late fourteenth century

speculate on the chill contrast between the huge sword, and the young lives which for reasons of State were cut off so prematurely. Within the Department of Medieval and Later Antiquities, it is possible to bridge in the imagination the gap which exists between a constitutional study of the English monarchy, and emotional contemplation of the grisly fate of the Princes of the Tower. Historical reality is here presented on an altar of great richness and beauty.

Chapter Nine

Western Asiatic Antiquities

Peter Young

In the days when I was in the army the British officer was a great traveller. I spent several years in the Middle East and saw the Acropolis, the Pyramids and the Old City of Jerusalem. I was lucky as I was also able to visit Petra – the 'rose-red city half as old as time' – Jerash, Um-el-Jimal, Megiddo, Acre, Sebastia and so on. I suppose I can claim to know Jerash and Jerusalem pretty well. The Acropolis and the Pyramids are not in fact in the area covered by the Department of Western Asiatic Antiquities, but, of course, the British Museum's division of the ancient world must be an arbitrary one. Obviously, Egyptian culture affected that of the Assyrians, who in turn influenced the Persians, from whom the Greeks derived many of their ideas. Nor was the heritage a purely cultural one, Greek, Persian and Assyrian in turn inherited ideas about military organization and tactics from the Empires that they had overthrown.

My choice of subjects for discussion is bound to be arbitrary, if only because of the *embarras de richesse* in the British Museum's collection. The Western Asiatic Department is a treasure trove of antiquities of the Sumerians, Baby- lonians and Assyrians who once inhabited Iraq; the Persians whose borders coincided with those of modern Iran; the Canaanites, Phoenicians, Syrians and Israelites, who lived in 'the Fertile Crescent' of Syria, Palestine, Jordan and Lebanon. The Hittites and Urartians of modern Turkey and what was Armenia, are included, as well as the Arabs of the Yemen and Saudi Arabia. Oddly enough the Carthaginians of distant Tunisia are included. When it is realized that the Department covers, roughly speaking, the period 5000 B.C. to the seventh century A.D., and the treasures of a dozen civilizations, its vast scope will at once be appreciated.

Rather to my surprise I find that some of the ancient masterpieces which interest me have nothing to do with war at all. I refer particularly to some of the treasures found at Ur of the Chaldees, but I will touch on these later. Let the human-headed winged lion of Ashurnasirpal II's Palace serve to introduce the collection. It is more than 2800 years old (1).

The animal portion of these great beasts with their numerous legs, seem to me well observed. Their curious, elaborate knotted girths are worth notice, as indeed is the elaborate hair-style of the human heads.

They come from a doorway in the Palace of Ashurnasirpal II (721–705 B.C.) at Nimrud. Beyond may be seen a reconstruction of the gates of Shalmaneser III. It was an old Sumerian custom to adorn the entrances of temples with paintings or frescoes of animals, especially lions or bulls, in order to drive away evil. It is thought that Shalmaneser I (*c.* 1260 B.C.), or one of his dynasty, was the first to decorate the gates of Assyrian palaces, as the Hittites had done, with these formidable defenders.

> But not only lions are used in this position. Thus, at Carchemish on the Euphrates, a part was found of at least one human-headed, bearded, gateway-lion, while the Syrian provincial ruler's palace at Tell Halaf, perhaps of the tenth century B.C., has female sphinxes, griffins, and a scorpion-man carved in the round in its doorways. Assyrian palaces, however, prefer as their gateway-figures human-headed, bearded, and winged lions or bulls.*

In one of the frescoes in the Nineveh Gallery we see gangs of slaves hauling a stone bull on a sledge. Some are laying timbers ahead to form a corduroy track, while others are bringing up two-wheeled carts with further supplies, cut doubt-less from the coniferous trees to be seen in the distance. This particular colossus, or *lamassâte*, was quarried by order of Sennacherib from the cliff at Balatai for the gateways of his palace at Nineveh. There is some charming detail in this particular frieze. In Barnett's words: 'Two men in a coracle bring great bronze or wooden loops for the gateposts; a man draws water (no doubt to wet the ropes) from a well by means of a *shadûf*, a type of counter-weighted arm still used at wells in the East; a wild sow with a row of piglets hides in the tall marsh-reeds.' The piglets are reminiscent of the animals one finds in a medieval book of hours or the Luttrell Psalter. There are about a dozen soldiers to be seen, at least eight of them are waving their arms about by way of showing their zeal – a typical military scene in fact.

Let us now return in time to Ur, the city of the ancient Sumerians which was flourishing in 2500 B.C., and to some of the treasures discovered by the archaeo-logist Sir Leonard Woolley in 1927. When I first saw the Goat and the Tree (2) I thought the animal was caught in the branches, but, it seems, he is merely rearing up to sniff at the flowers. It is too easy to see some sinister meaning in the masterpieces of ancient art. This figure has a companion in the University Museum at Philadelphia. It has been deduced from the tubes between their shoulders that they supported a piece of furniture. They had some symbolic significance, probably mythological, but though the motif of two goats about the Sacred Tree is common in Mesopotamian art, its precise meaning is not known.

This handsome beast has a face and legs of gold-leaf, eyes, horns and shoulder

* R. D. Barnett, *Assyrian Palace Reliefs*, p. 10.

1. The human-headed winged lion from the Palace of Ashurnasirpal II (883–859 B.C.)
at Nimrud

fleece of lapis lazuli, and body fleece of white shell. The Sacred Tree is of gold leaf. Could Fabergé have done better?

Queen Pu-abi's golden bowl was found with a silver drinking-tube or 'straw', at her bedside in the Royal Cemetery of Ur. The cup (3) and the goblet came from the death-pit at the entrance to her grave. They were found with two other gold vessels and the remains of the Queen's wardrobe chest. The bowl is boat-shaped and quite plain except for the lugs to secure the twisted gold wire by which it was suspended.

Queen Pu-abi's lyre (4), also from the 'Great Death Pit' at Ur, is certainly one of the oldest musical instruments in existence, and perhaps one of the most handsome. It was found with the bodies of male and female servants in the entrance to Queen Pu-abi's tomb, and had to be reconstructed. It is now thought to need some modification. However that may be, it has beautiful features:

> The front of the sounding-board is ornamented with a splendid bull's head made of gold sheet hammered over a wooden core, with beard and mane of lapis lazuli; his collar and the edging of the sound-box is inlaid with lively scenes of the lion-headed eagle (Im-dugud) clawing at two goats, two bulls nibbling at two trees, a bull-man wrestling with two leopards, and a lion seizing a bull.*

Some of the oldest head-dresses in existence come from Ur. They are both beautiful and practical, and they resemble the *kaffiyeh* and the *agal*, head-dresses used by modern Arab men and women, inhabiting the same part of the world, to keep off heat and cold.

This head-dress (5) has a delicate jewelled crown to keep it in place. The leaves of the decoration resemble those of the beech which can scarcely have been native to Ur of the Chaldees. Where, one wonders, had the artist seen a leaf of this species.

But much as I enjoy these treasures I find my thoughts turning once more to warfare. Practically every aspect of the art of war in ancient times is illustrated in the Assyrian palace reliefs.

The Assyrian Empire, having no natural frontiers, depended for survival upon its army, which for nearly 300 years was remarkably efficient. Its triumphs were celebrated in the sculptures and bronzes which adorned the palaces of Nineveh. They give us a great deal of significant detail, much in the way that the Bayeux Tapestry tells us of the army of William the Conqueror. At the Battle of Qarqar in 854 B.C., Shalmaneser III commanded an army that is said to have been 120,000 strong. Though ancient statistics may be suspect this argues a *levée en masse* of the manpower of the Empire. The Assyrians,

* R. D. Barnett, *Fifty Masterpieces of Ancient Near Eastern Art*, p. 11.

2. The Goat and the Tree

3. Queen Pu-abi's gold feeding-cup,
from Ur; c. 2500 B.C.

however, warred far afield and the core of their army was evidently composed of
professional soldiers. In addition they formed units from among their captives.

The Assyrian army was capable either of open or siege warfare. It had chariots,
cavalry, foot-soldiers, a battering-train, pontoons and a rudimentary supply
service. All these are illustrated in the reliefs.

In a pitched battle the chariot corps, equivalent perhaps to the armoured cars
and tanks of modern armies, was the principal strength of the army. Over the
years, the design of the chariot was considerably modified. Under Ashurnasirpal it had three horses; later, under Shalmaneser III only two. Eighty years
later Tiglath-pileser III made the vehicle heavier, but it was still light enough to
be carried in emergency by two men.

In early times, the crew was two men; a driver and a bowman. Later, in
Sargon's time, the crew was increased to three, the third man carrying two round
shields with which to protect the driver and the archer.

Finally, in the days of Ashurbanipal, 200 years later, the crew rose to four,
with the addition of a second shield-bearer, and the chariot, of course, had to
be made heavier. The crew were now practically mounted infantry.

The Assyrian cavalry consisted of mounted archers and spearmen, though the
former sometimes carried spears as well. I suspect that the cavalry shown here
were 'regulars' for they wear the characteristic Assyrian conical helmet. In any

case it takes a long time to train cavalry and so irregulars would not be much use. The Assyrians did not have stirrups and for this reason shock action cannot have been very attractive. The saddles were rudimentary, nothing more than a sort of quilt. Even so Sennacherib's cavalry presented a smart appearance, the men all dressed the same, and their sturdy, alert-looking horses, each with his long tail plaited and with a plume at his throat. The horses seem to have been well schooled for they are standing still to let their riders take aim. But Assyrian cavalry, like Red Indians, who also had no use for stirrups, were capable of shooting as they cantered to the charge.

Cavalry of this sort, despite the fact that they wore helmets and some armour, can scarcely be compared with the heavy and medium cavalry of later times. One can only assume, therefore, that they were used for patrols, reconnaissance and work on the flanks, when the army was in battle.

The infantry was armed for missile or shock action. The missiles were bow

4. Silver lyre from the 'Great Death Pit' at Ur; c. 2500 B.C.

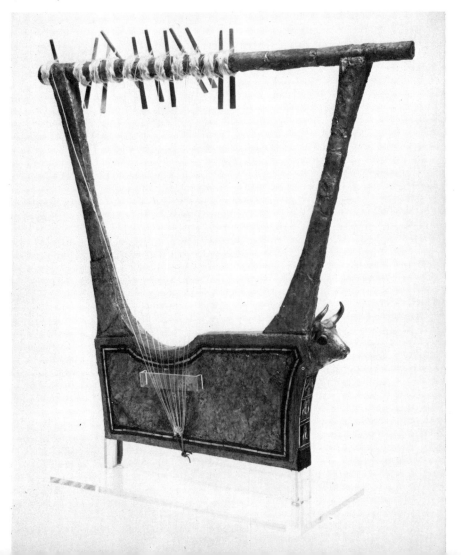

or sling, and the main shock weapon was the spear. The spearmen in their coats of mail and carrying wicker shields cannot have been very mobile.

Some of the archers, probably the Assyrian regulars, wore armour, but others, no doubt recruited from conquered nations, and therefore expendable, were not even issued with shields.

The slingers, though they did not have shields, were in other respects equipped like the Assyrian archers. Their range seems to have been at least comparable with that of the composite bow, and their rate of fire was probably just as rapid.

The main siege engine was the battering-ram. One from the reign of Ashur-banirpal bears a remarkable resemblance to a Dalek. It had six wheels and was, therefore, probably quite heavy. Its sides seem to be made of overlapping wicker shields. The domed observation-post, like a rudimentary tank turret is a nice touch. The ram itself is probably made of a tree-trunk shod with a metal head. A rather cruder engine with its ram shaped like a boar's head, had a pole at the rear no doubt so that it could be pulled on the march by draught animals.

Then as now foresight, intelligence, surprise and the use of ground, were factors that tipped the scale, even when a general had numbers against him. The Assyrian army is of special interest because of its organizational and tactical ideas from which Persia, and, in turn, ancient Greece, were to profit.

In 700 B.C. the army of Sennacherib by-passed Jerusalem and fell upon the key fortress of Lachish in southern Palestine (Judea), now called the Tel ed Duweir. King Hezekiah, who had 'rebelled against the king of Assyria, and served him not', was shut up 'like a caged bird' in Jerusalem. The reliefs which Sir Austen Layard discovered at Nineveh (1847) are, in the opinion of Professor Yadin, 'one of the most important 'war documents' on battle in Judah'. They reveal the tactics and weapons of the defenders. The broad sequence of the events of the siege are clearly revealed. In the first phase slingers, and archers headed by spearmen with round shields, assail the city with their missiles. All the bowmen seem to be armed with the same weapon, but there are two distinct 'uniforms'. The familiar Assyrian regulars have their characteristic conical helmet (not unlike those worn in the Middle Ages by the followers of William the Conqueror), and their tunic of mail, as do the slingers (6). The other half of the archers, no doubt some sort of auxiliaries, have no armour. The spearmen have helmets with a crescent-shaped crest. The slingers stand behind the archers, which might be taken to indicate that their weapons were not out-ranged by the short bows of their comrades. The sling is the weapon of the nomadic shepherd, who can direct and guide his flock by dropping stones in front of the leading beast. When I commanded the 9th Regiment of the Arab Legion in Jerusalem in 1954, I was occasionally plagued by complaints from the Mixed Armistice Commission that my soldiers had hit Jewish sentries

5. Head-dress from Ur; gold, lapis lazuli and carnelian; c. 2500 B.C.

6. Slingers at the siege of Lachish from a relief from the Palace of Sennacherib (704–681 B.C.) at Nineveh

with stones thrown from the walls of the Old City. This I denied with a clear conscience for the range was something like 100 yards, and the idea was there-fore patently absurd. But my confidence was somewhat disturbed when I learned later that some of my soldiers still had their shepherd's slings. . . .

This is a soldier of Sennacherib's (705–681 B.C.) army, and from his shield and helmet I deduce that he is a regular. This relief illustrates the Assyrians' ingenuity in crossing rivers. Some of the men are shown blowing up their goat-skins on the bank, while others are swimming across, with their shields and weapons on their backs to keep them dry – a point which illustrates their good discipline. In No. 3 Commando in the Second World War we used to practise river crossing in the same fashion, but using our gas-capes and groundsheets. We were not issued with goatskins.

The Assyrians could get their chariots across rivers either by pontoon-bridges in the case of small streams, or by ferrying them in large boats, propelled by oars

7. The capitulation of the Elamites at the Battle of the River Ulai from reliefs of Ashurbanipal (668–627 B.C.) from Nineveh (*above*)

8. Ashurbanipal celebrating his victory over Te-umman and the Elamites at the River Ulai; from a relief from his Palace at Nineveh (*below*)

and at the same time hauled by the advanced guard with ropes. The horses swam behind, each with a groom in the boat to hold his halter.

The reliefs show the assault phase of the siege. The fortress was evidently taken by escalade, the storming-parties consisting of both spearmen and bow-men, the latter drawn from among the armoured archers. They were nimble fellows for they shot their arrows even while climbing the scaling-ladders. The slingers did not go into the assault, it seems, for they can be seen giving covering-fire. Battering-rams advanced along ramps of logs or mud-brick, headed some of the assault-parties, while the defenders rained down lighted torches.

The lot of the prisoners was hard. Some were impaled, some flayed alive and those whose lives were spared were either enlisted or set to forced labour.

The relief of the last phase shows the Assyrians removing their spoils on camels and in ox-carts, while the King, enthroned before his pavilion and fanned by attendants, examines some of the prisoners who humble themselves before him. Near by, his chariot, drawn by vigorous horses, awaits his pleasure.

Though Sennacherib triumphed at Lachish he failed to take Jerusalem. In 2 Kings 18–20 you may read of the 'Danegelt' that Hezekiah gave him, the negotiations that went on, the brave words of Isaiah the Prophet, and how 'the angel of the Lord went out and smote in the camp of the Assyrians an hundred fourscore and five thousand: and when they arose early in the morning, behold, they were all dead corpses.' So Sennacherib departed, and as the Prophet had foretold, the virgin daughter of Zion laughed him to scorn. 'And it came to pass, as he was worshipping in the house of Nisroch his god, that Adrammelech

9. Ashurbanipal routing the Arabs; from a relief from his Palace at Nineveh

10. Ashurbanipal hunting lions; from a relief from his Palace at Nineveh

and Sharezer his sons smote him with the sword: and they escaped into the land of Armenia. And Esarhaddon his son reigned in his stead' – but not until 681 B.C.

The Battle of the River Ulai (653 B.C.) had been described as Ashurbani-pal's 'crowning mercy'. In it he defeated the Babylonians and the Elamites, and great was the slaughter (7). He commemorated his triumph in boldly executed reliefs.

It has been suggested that the Assyrian official war artist may have accom-panied the expeditionary force to Egypt and been influenced by what he saw there.

The Elamites are shown in flagrant rout. Their soldiers include a few scattered riders, light archers and other foot, and additionally a number of vehicles: carts with a high platform and big wheels with twelve or sixteen spokes, and chariots, built on the same lines, with eight-spoked wheels. The pursuing Assyrians are cavalry, armed with bow or spear, and infantry armed with spears and light bows. They wear the characteristic conical helmet. Some have wicker shields covered with leather, and strengthened by a central metal boss. In the best strip-cartoon tradition, the reliefs show several phases of the fight, from the initial assault to the decapitation of the prisoners, but everywhere the Elamites are in disorder, rushing down a steep slope, being thrust into the Ulai, which is full of dead men and horses, with numerous fish and an enormous crab thrown in for good measure. Here men are seen crushed beneath the wheels of a vehicle, there an Elamite bowman pierced by an arrow begs an Assyrian soldier to finish him off. King Te͵umman hemmed in by half a dozen foes draws his bow against them, while his son kneels beside him, unarmed and begging for mercy.

Ashurbanipal celebrated his victory with a feast under the vines of his royal garden (8). He reclines on a divan, drinking with his consort, who sits on a high throne, while attendants fan them. With remarkable bad taste, the severed head of the unfortunate Te͵umman has been suspended near by, as if from a hat͵stand – actually from a neighbouring tree.

The Assyrian palace reliefs also show Ashurbanipal's campaign against the Arabs (9). The practically naked Bedu as yet without the *kaffiyeh* and the robes of T. E. Lawrence's day, are no match for the Assyrian regulars with their helmets and composite (reinforced) bows. Small wonder that they are belting back to the Sahara as fast as their camels will carry them! Incidentally camels don't gallop leading with both forelegs, but otherwise they are beautifully observed. It was a bright idea to have one Arab driving with his camel͵stick, and another 'riding shotgun', if one may use the expression – shooting Parthian shots over the camel's tail. They didn't do that in the Arab Legion. One pair has come to grief, it's not quite clear why, but, of course, once they can get clear the camels will soon outpace the Assyrian archers' horses – at least I hope so.

A fragment of another relief from Ashurbanipal's palace at Nineveh shows his soldiers sacking and burning tents and spearing the unfortunate Arabs – a scene that recalls the famous night raid near Beisan, when the field͵word was 'the sword of the Lord and of Gideon'.

The reliefs in Ashurbanipal's palace at Nineveh celebrate not only his triumphs in war but his achievements in the chase. The scenes of lion͵hunting (10) are even better than the battle͵pieces and have rightly been described as 'the high water mark of ancient Near Eastern narrative art'. Naturally, they show the King in an heroic light, dispatching lions single͵handed with an air of truly monumental sang͵froid.

It was not to be expected that the King – whose hunting͵kit was highly unsuitable for any violent activity – would seek the lion in the jungle of the Meso͵ potamian river marshes. The poor beasts were first netted and caged and then released when the King felt like hunting – rather in the way that the German Electors of the early eighteenth century shot the stag. That these are real rather than ritual scenes is shown not only by the beautiful and sympathetic treatment of the stricken lions, but by the group of Ninevite peasants watching from a near͵by hill.

The brilliant sculptor's feeling for the animals is very evident, and makes clear his dislike of this unfair sport in a stiff portrayal of his arrogant patron.

Chapter Ten

Oriental Antiquities

Malcolm MacDonald

I first became attracted by antique Oriental works of art when I was a university student. One of their qualities which enticed me – a dour Scot – was their exotic character. They presented to me peoples, ideas and beliefs that seemed very different from anything I had known before. They were novel; they were mysterious. I wanted to learn about the strange civilizations which produced them. So I used to go to the British Museum to glimpse its Asian art treasures, and try to supplement my admiration with understanding of what inspired them. Later, I had the good fortune to live for many years in Eastern lands, getting to know as friends the Chinese, Japanese, Indians, Thais, Cambodians and other peoples whose ancestors made those graceful things, and who still valued the influence of their ancient cultures.

Most of them were gentle, shy characters; or perhaps they were just enigmatic to a stranger, for when one broke through their reserve they became enchantingly friendly. Then they talked with intimate and often scholarly knowledge about the traditional customs, religious faiths, ethical codes and other legacies which had been handed down to them through centuries. I viewed examples of their ancient architecture, sculptures, paintings and other arts in their proper settings, and found that some of the skills which produced them still lived, having passed from father to son among local artists and craftsmen. The wood-carvers in Bali, batik-makers in Java and silversmiths in many different countries produced superbly beautiful objects that matched the creations of their ancestors.

A rich variety of relics from those Oriental civilizations are lodged in the British Museum. I cannot claim to be an erudite authority on them; I am an amateur connoisseur who likes things that please the eye regardless of their antiquity or rarity value. In the Far East, my taste skipped from one type of art to another – painting, sculpture, ceramics, bronzes and so on – distributed in one Oriental country after another – China, India, Cambodia, Persia and many more.

As fine and probably as old as any civilization in the world is that of China. The bronze ritual vessel (1) was made about the year 1100 B.C. The Emperors of the first historically recorded dynasty – the Shang – had already been ruling for more than three centuries in the Valley of the Yellow River, which was the

1. Ritual vessel (Tsun); bronze; China; twelfth-eleventh century B.C.

cradle of Chinese culture. They believed that earthly affairs were governed by the spirits of their ancestors and other superhuman beings; and to gain the favour of those deities they periodically offered them sacrifices with great pomp and ceremony. This vessel was a jar to hold wine for the spirits which could be poured out when the moment came on those sacred occasions to quench their thirsts. It is formidably handsome, standing almost two feet high; and the figures of rams adorning it fulfil three functions – symbolism, utility and aesthetic grace. Live rams were sacrificial animals; their images on this jar acted as efficient handles; and those horned and bearded heads give the cup ornate artistic distinction.

Craftsmen of the Shang period produced works fashioned in various other materials, but their artistic genius found its fullest expression in bronze ritual vessels, many of which were used in burial ceremonies and have been subsequently uncovered by archaeologists. It was the period of the Bronze Age in

Western parts of the world as well as in the East, and the artistic creations of those very different regions were, to some extent, mutually influenced as a result of communications along routes used sometimes by traders and at other times by invading armies.

No people have excelled the Chinese in the variety as well as the brilliance of their arts. Throughout almost all the 3000 years since the Shang ruled they have evolved a succession of styles in sculpture, painting, ceramics, jade, textiles and all manner of other substances. For example, the Chinese were great potters. During their Tang dynasty, which lasted for 300 years after A.D. 618, they made figures of horses, ducks, camels (2) and contemporary characters like musicians, dancing-girls and servants that were buried in the grave of some lord so that they could continue looking after him in his next life. Of course, the potters were just as anxious to help the living in this world as their spirits in the next. The British Museum has one of the finest collections on display anywhere in the Western world of dishes, vases, teapots, wine-cups and ornaments from Imperial palaces, mandarins' mansions and the poorer homes in every successive dynasty through the long history of Old Cathay.

Many of these objects provide a valuable insight into the Chinese character. Take, for example, the white porcelain figurine of Kuan-yin, the Chinese goddess of mercy, made in the eighteenth century (3). No image could be more

2. Camel; pottery with coloured glazes; China; eighth century A.D.

3. The saviour goddess, Kuan-yin; white porcelain; China; eighteenth century A.D.

4. *Autumn Scene*; colour on paper; China by K'un-ts'an (active A.D. 1657–74)

gracefully, serenely, exquisitely lovely than she! In a near-by case stands an
almost contemporary group showing a European family of a father, mother and
two children fashioned in the same type of porcelain. By comparison with the
Kuan-yin they appear very loutish! And they represent not so much the difference, in Chinese eyes, between divine and human beings, as between Chinese
and European mortals. The Chinese regarded themselves as civilized, while
viewing all other peoples as 'barbarians'.

Look at this delicately coloured painting by one of the best artists of the Ching
dynasty (4). He was a monk – and most of the time a hermit – named K'un-
ts'an who wielded his brush in the seventeenth century. It is one of a set of pictures representing the Four Seasons. Of course, this autumn scene has for us
Westerners an unfamiliar, exotic, even mysterious quality. Can such a landscape really be a correct interpretation of nature? As a matter of fact it is; I have
often gazed with awe on such sights in China. Nevertheless, it is true that many
Chinese artists were inclined to let their imaginations run riot, to idealize
reality. Moreover, they often sought to sketch with their brushes something more
complex than an ordinary painting. The poem floating in the space where the
sky should be in K'un-ts'an's picture, and the decorative calligraphy in which
those verses are written, make it a representation of three types of art combined in
one piece.

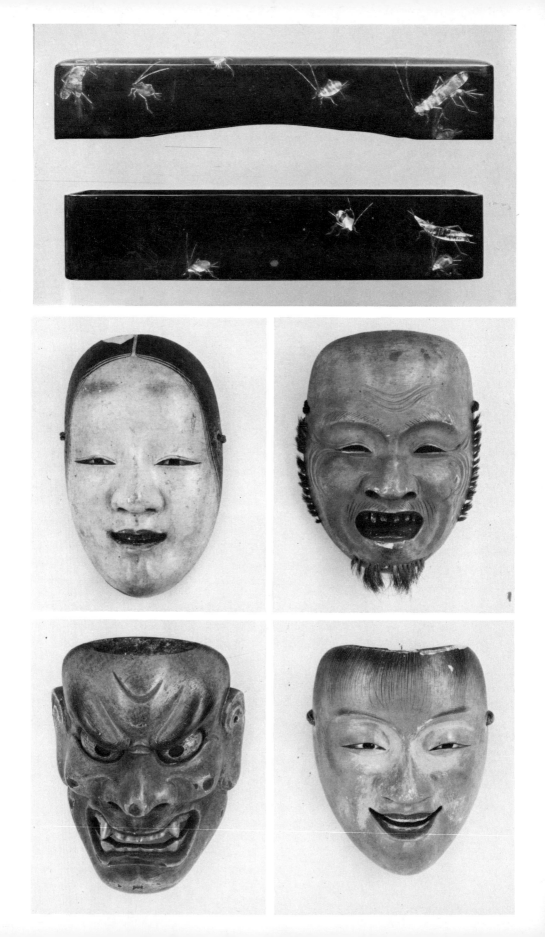

7. Head of an old man; stucco; Afghanistan; fifth century A.D.

The Japanese also have a tradition of superb artistry. This lacquer box (5) was made about the year A.D. 1200 for holding scroll documents. The technical skill with which the mother-of-pearl is inlaid and the silver lacquer applied on the black could not be finer. If you see it in the Museum, note the grace and delicacy of the grasshoppers and crickets jumping round the box lid. They demonstrate that man's imitations of God's creations can attain their own perfection.

Through the centuries, the Japanese fashioned many exquisite styles of lacquer; and they still do so today. I have watched humble craftsmen squatting on the floors in their small workshops in the ancient capital of Kyoto applying patiently layer upon layer, over many months, the black, gilt and other-hued lacquers which gradually create one of these rich works of art.

I never tire of looking at Japanese paintings, either the delicately imaginative early water-colours created for the appreciation of intellectual aristocrats, or the later woodcuts made for the enjoyment of the more ordinary populace which reveal vividly the gaily costumed characters and quaint scenes of everyday life in seventeenth-, eighteenth- and nineteenth-century Japan.

Throughout the ages the Asians have been great lovers of dancing and drama.

5. Document box; lacquer and mother-of-pearl; Japan; c. A.D. 1200 (opposite above)

6. Masks for the No and Kyogen dramas; lacquered wood; Japan; eighteenth century A.D. (opposite below)

8. The Conception of the Buddha; Schist; West Pakistan; second-third century A.D.

Some of the most gracious, decorative, fabulous theatricals that I have ever watched were performed in different lands in the Far East. The traditional Chinese opera, the Kathakali performances in Kerala in southern India, the ballets as well as the shadow plays of Java, and the temple dances in Bali are just a few examples of the gorgeous masks still enacted today, often with the same costumes, the same steppings and the same music that have enthralled audiences through many centuries. The motives inspiring those Oriental spectacles are varied. They may be acts of homage to the gods aimed to provide the human audience with a moral lesson.

The Japanese have always been devotees of the theatre. Long before most of them could read or write, the people learned from stage performances about the myths, legends and historical episodes which played significant parts in shaping their national character, beliefs and way of life. The most famous of their traditional dramas were the No and Kyogen plays. Every detail of the costumes worn, the words spoken and the gestures made by the actors became stereo-

10. Siva as Teacher (Dakshimamurti);
Granite; South India; c. A.D. 950

typed as early as the fourteenth century, changing scarcely at all during the next 500 years. The picture (6) shows four out of scores of different kinds of masks worn by players. This quartet represent a wrathful god, a tipsy Chinese fairy, a grim ghost and a pure young virgin. You can imagine the abiding impression which those eloquent faces made on children, peasants and other simple folk who watched them playing their didactic parts in the glare of footlights.

The civilization of the Indian subcontinent can claim one of the longest histories of all. In the Indus Valley a remarkably advanced society flourished as early as the third millennium B.C. The illustration of a fragment of Gandhara sculpture (7) comes from Afghanistan and dates from the fifth century A.D. There is a touch of Classical Mediterranean influence in its otherwise Oriental character. Alexander the Great carried his conquests as far east as northern India, leaving behind him when he departed not only Macedonian governors and troops but also Hellenistic craftsmen. Many authorities regard Gandhara sculptures as Indo-Greek, though others believe that the foreign influence came rather later, being more Roman than Greek. Nevertheless, all the Gand-

11. *Krishna and the Milkmaids*; Gouache on paper; the Panjab Hills; Basohli school;
c. A.D. 1720

hara works are fundamentally Indian. This stone panel (8), for example, shows
the Buddha's mother, Queen Maya, lying asleep. She is dreaming that a white
elephant descends upon her, and you can see that sacred animal floating in the
air above her couch. However, legend declares that her dream became reality
and that as a result of the elephant's visit she gave birth to the Buddha.

Buddhism existed in India alongside the more ancient Brahminism with its multitude of Hindu gods and goddesses. Eminent among those deities was Siva, who possessed many talents. The British Museum displays a superb granite carving of him as a Yoga teacher (10). It is one of the noblest pieces of Indian sculpture outside India and belongs to the tenth century – the best period of south Indian religious art.

Siva also appeared in the guise of lord of the dance. The bronze illustrated here (9) shows him in that character. This graceful figure surrounded by a halo of flames was cast about the year A.D. 930, and is probably the earliest of its type still surviving anywhere in the world.

Siva possessed phenomenal strength. Legend relates that a certain group of human sages lived in such pious austerity that the gods feared they would compete with them by acquiring divine powers. Siva and his colleague Vishnu therefore went to interrupt their meditations, and so to weaken them. In self-defence the sages created a tiger, a snake, a demon and a fire to frustrate the deities. But Siva conquered all those ferocious phenomena. He slew the tiger and used its skin as a garment. He wrapped the snake round his wrist as a bracelet, confined the fire in a small bowl and crushed the demon by dancing on it – as is shown in this bronze.

Painting was another field in which the Indians achieved great distinction. Among the finest of their creations are magnificent groups of figures decorating the walls of Buddhist cave-temples that were cut into massive cliffs at Ajanta. They were made between the second century B.C. and the eighth century A.D. The British Museum does not possess any of those classic Indian works of art, which can only be viewed in their original rock homes. But it owns paintings from a later period in Indian history. After the conquest of vast areas of the subcontinent by Muslim invaders from the thirteenth century onwards, Islamic culture made an important contribution to the development of Indian and Pakistani civilization. The most celebrated of the Muslim rulers were the Mughal Emperors of the sixteenth and seventeenth centuries, who came from central Asia and brought with them Persian ideas about architecture and painting. The miniature paintings made in their regal courts are as beautiful as they are famous. But although the original inspiration of those miniatures was Persian, local Hindu craftsmen had to be employed to execute them, and they quite naturally used traditional Indian techniques and concepts. So as time passed, Persian characteristics gradually disappeared, and they became increasingly Indian in spirit and character.

The miniature pictured here (11) is of the early eighteenth century and was probably painted in the small State of Basohli in the Himalayan foothills. It portrays the much-loved Hindu deity Krishna dallying with his mistress Radha

12. The future Buddha, Maitreya; Gilt-copper; Nepal; ninth-tenth century A.D. (*left*)

13. The saviour goddess, Tara; Gilt-bronze; Ceylon; tenth century A.D. (*right*)

attended by two other favourites among the milkmaids. Its style shows how these miniatures had evolved from primarily Persian to wholly Indian expressions of life.

From the early centuries of Christianity, India's political, cultural and religious influences spread far beyond its own borders, crossing the frontier into Nepal and neighbouring lands, and the sea into Ceylon and various parts of South-East Asia.

A Nepalese gilt-copper figure of about the year 900 shows the Maitreya Buddha (12) who in the next life-circle will follow the historical Gautama

14. Ewer; brass inlaid with silver and copper; made at Mosul in A.D. 1232

Buddha. Seated with majestic serenity, he holds his hands in the gesture of instruction.

And look at this slightly later Ceylonese portrayal of the goddess Tara (13), who was a Bodhisattva or Saviour Deity, a compassionate being who could rescue mortals from material or spiritual distress. Dignified and benevolent, she stands nearly five feet tall. She is one of the Museum's principal treasures.

Talented societies thrived in Burma, Cambodia and Java, and in those lands magnificent architectural and other relics from medieval times still survive. No more impressive group of ancient monuments exists anywhere than the palaces, temples and other grand edifices in the jungle at Angkor in Cambodia. The brilliant Khmer people who raised them were geniuses in sculpture as well as architecture. They portrayed in many of their statues the sublime physical beauty and spiritual calm of their ladies, qualities that still characterize many women all over South-East Asia today.

Indeed, one reason why I felt happy during my years among the peoples of South-East Asia two decades ago was that they still preserved in their conduct

15. Mosque lamp; pottery with underglaze decoration; Turkey; dated A.D. 1549

16. Carved, wooden hornbill; Borneo

and attitudes some of the best features of their ancient cultures. For instance, many of them attached more importance to the spiritual elements in life than to the material values which industrialized Western nations were beginning to think more worshipful. Those Asians lived a more relaxed, sometimes lackadaisical existence. They were mentally alert but spiritually calm, and did not chase hectically after immense commercial profits and industrial gains. Nor had they huge factories filled with regiments of machines. Their clothes, household goods and artistic ornaments were still made individually by the hands of trained craftsmen instead of by mechanical, mass-production processes. And their finest works of art were usually created as acts of worship of local deities and therefore had to be of superlative beauty if those gods were not to be offended.

But in the last twenty years what is called 'modern progress' has destroyed not only certain conservative customs which were no doubt better consigned to the dustbins of history, but also many ethical concepts and artistic skills, the disappearance of which is an irreparable loss to mankind.

The other cultures represented in the Department of Oriental Antiquities are those which thrived in the Islamic lands in the Near East from the seventh century A.D. onwards.

As a devotee of ceramics, I think the finest potters after the Chinese were the Islamic peoples of that region. They made a great variety of wares throughout the Middle Ages and later, and these are well represented in the collection. The

Turkish mosque lamp illustrated (15) is one of the Museum's finest examples of Islamic pottery.

One of the Museum's most enviable treasures is this ewer (14). Originally, it had a long tapering spout, which somehow, sometime, got broken, and disap-peared. Otherwise it remains in superb condition. Its brass surface is decorated with inlaid silver and copper as well as engraving. Scenes of Court life are set in polygonal frames, their subjects including a prince enthroned, a horseman hunting with a cheetah, musicians playing tuneful instruments, battle scenes, and courtiers feasting and drinking.

The band running round the lower part of the ewer's shoulder is composed of animals, birds and human figures intricately arranged to form Arabic words, while other bands are inscribed in Arabic script, including one giving the name of the piece's maker, and the date and place of its creation. Made at Mosul by Shuja 'ibn Man'a in the year A.D. 1232, it is probably the best product of that city's metal-workers.

A wing of the gallery which houses Islamic antiquities contained until recently samples of arts and crafts made in modern times by natives of South-East Asia. Although they belong to the Museum's Ethnographical Department (Burling-ton Gardens), I venture to illustrate one of them here, for it shows that creating beauty is not the prerogative of sophisticated peoples. This decorative wood-carving of a bird called the 'hornbill' (16), which in real life inhabits the jungles of Sarawak and gobbles in its colossal beak grasshoppers, lizards, berries and other foodstuffs, is an example of the present-day work of Iban tribesmen there – some of the notorious 'Wild men of Borneo'. Their favourite sport until a few years ago was head-hunting. I have never enjoyed myself more than when I used to stay with those characterful, charming and capable people in their long-houses in the tropical forests. I watched them using their sharp knives not to cut off heads but to carve creatures like this engaging hornbill, and images of the wild animals, hobgoblins and other good and evil spirits who haunt their animist world.

Thirty thousand years ago our forebears in Europe, also primitive tribesmen, painted splendid pictures in caves, like those at Lascaux. I have seen Eskimos squatting in their igloos on the frozen Arctic Ocean carving beautiful soapstone figurines of seals, snowy owls, loons and other local creatures; and have gazed at lovely rock-paintings made only yesterday by the nomadic Bushmen of southern Africa; and have watched the wild Kenyah tribesmen in Borneo step-ping head-hunter dances with a grace of movement as unforgettably sublime as a classic Russian ballet. One of the many enlightening lessons that the galleries in the British Museum teach us is that all men, from all epochs and all lands, are brothers in their capacity to create and cherish noble works of art.

Chapter Eleven

Ethnography

David Stafford-Clark

The human race is the most recent, complex and original form of life known on this planet. In terms of the evolution of the human brain, that finally decisive asset which distinguishes man from every other living creature, our history goes back a million years.

Ethnography is the descriptive study of human cultures, and is limited by our present knowledge to the latter half of man's evolution as a separate species. Actual traces of human culture go back little further than 500,000 years; and the earliest evidence of that culture may be the Acheulian handaxe, which is either a weapon or an agricultural tool; or the eoliths, dawn stones chipped from rocks.

What does all this mean? It means that our human history is but an eye-blink in cosmic time as astronomers reckon it. Caldwell, the quietly desperate peda-gogue in John Updike's novel *The Centaur*, sought to inspire his stubbornly recalcitrant class by accelerating the time process; this he did by setting the beginning of time as we know it, with the emergence of the planet Earth and the whole of the galactic systems of the stars which surround it, a mere three days ago. Given that explosively vivid condensation of conceptual time, where-by our universe began at noon three days ago from the time that you read this, then man emerged only one minute after midday today. In this way, man's life as a species is seen in proportion against the backdrop of cosmic time; whereby a minute has become the equivalent of a million years. Ethnography as an art and a science began, in this context, no more than an infinite decimal fraction of a second ago; and it is a discipline that concerns itself only with the last half-minute of existence.

No one can say how this tremendous cultural explosion, man's emergence as a thinking creature, has come to pass in such a minute fraction of the history of the universe. All we know is that our million-year heritage has given us the chance to emerge from a purely animal existence into one in which we can look before and after, can reckon not only with our own existence in the present, but with the history of our past and the probabilities of our future. The strange thing is that the study of man in his cultural setting began only a hundred years ago. Long before that, poets had conceived the necessity of such a study:

Mexican serpent mask, probably representing Quetzalcoatl

Know then thyself, presume not God to scan,
The proper study of mankind is Man.

Alexander Pope (1688–1744) included that memorable observation in his *Essay on Man*, but scientists of his day were still too busy studying the material universe about them to recognize that they themselves were part of that universe, and that their actions and discoveries were even then acting upon the very circumstances which they were studying, and influencing the future which we, over 200 years later, would inherit.

Ethnography embraces such fundamental matters as the conquest of fire, the ability to shape and use tools and weapons, the recognition of the power of ritual for learning, warning and conveying significance among tribes and cultures of men and women; and such epochal but mechanically gigantic leaps forward as the discovery, and ultimately the use, of the wheel. (As recently as the seventeenth and eighteenth centuries, American Indians used hoops as toys, but dragged booty and bodies on wheel-less sleds.) One of the most fascinating rewards of the study of ethnography has been the recognition that perhaps every stage in man's cultural evolution is still present somewhere in the world today. There are still men and women living in a Stone Age culture of a kind in which many of our ancestors lived perhaps 5000 or even 10,000 years ago; and from which we in Britain had not emerged until some of the oldest

Acheulian hand-axe
from Gray's Inn Lane

Bronze grotesque head for the spirit cult; Late Period

and greatest civilizations which preceded ours in other parts of the world, such as Africa, Asia and the central and southern parts of the two American continents, had perished and disappeared as suddenly and mysteriously as they had arisen.

Ethnography is a dazzling corrective to conventional patterns of thought. Perhaps the first indication which I personally received of this was when I first travelled to Greece, with my schoolboy's impression that Greece was the source of human culture still intact. My awakening came when, in one of the main squares of Athens, I saw a large neon advertisement for Egyptian National Airlines which said simply and unequivocally 'Fly to Cairo, the Cradle of Civilization'. Nowadays, a smart public relations adviser to the Mexican or

Saron demong, an instrument (with metal keys) from the Raffles *Gamelan*; 39½ in

Guatemalan Airlines might put up a similar advertisement inviting travellers to inspect the remains of Mayan and Aztec civilizations.

The first question which might seem to confront us in looking at the ethno graphical collection of the British Museum is why it appears to be so random. It might even seem to be capricious, set against all those half million years between the beginnings of primitive culture and the present day; to lean, indeed, too heavily upon the last 5000 years; thereby yet again restricting itself almost arbitrarily to a hundredth of the period for which it could be held responsible. This would be to miss the whole point, both of the origins of ethnography, and of the basis on which selection must necessarily be made.

We must think of the time when men on voyages all over the world were collecting curios to bring home. Their collections were indeed arbitrary and capricious, although in some cases they were also locally complete within the field of their interest. The task of a Keeper at the British Museum was inescapably first to survey the available field in terms of the Museum's own potential collec tions, then to select for display primarily those closest to perfection and complete in themselves; without forgetting that the further back in history men venture, the fewer curios and relics are to be found.

But if the purpose of ethnographic collection is to give an inkling of how much may be learned, and of how much may surprise and delight; while inexorably at the same time confronting man with the nature of his brotherhood, the beauty of his work and the horror of his history of wars, massacres, human sacrifices, and their justification, then the present exhibition emerges as a spectacular triumph.

Look, for example, at the exhibits from the Benin collection illustrating the African idea of divine kingship, the social and political technique whereby mankind has sought both to have an unassailable order in his tribe and culture, and a supernatural scapegoat for otherwise incomprehensible natural catastrophes: a reason for floods, famines, earthquakes, tidal waves and volcanic eruptions. Herein he could construct a hierarchy of authority, and thereafter vest this finally in someone who could be seen but not touched, who was real,

Javanese shadow puppet (*wayang purwa*); showing Bima as a young man

human and alive as an acknowledged leader, but never without some attribute of divinity, some hint of supernatural power. Otherwise, regal authority risked becoming a matter of violent competition, of palace revolutions, of established order violently overthrown, to be replaced only by tyranny or ephemeral chaos.

Divine kingship as it is still known today in the Benin tribe in West Africa is precisely and beautifully documented in the exhibition. Its historical counter-part in Europe is the divine right of kings still ritually preserved in the coronation ceremonies of our own monarchy; and as intimately connected with the need for an earthly figure standing for an eternal reality as the Catholic concept of an infallible pope, vicar of Christ in Roman Catholicism for close on 2000 years.

Over the last million years are scattered examples of human activity that still survive somewhere even though to us they are remote in historical time. The Hadza Stone Age culture, for instance, is not less real today in Tanzania than astronauts and moon shots in America and Russia. If Hadza hunters and gatherers remind us of our past, while N A S A, Cape Kennedy and television invade our present, then ethnography remains ready to record our future. Even the Inter-Continental Ballistic Missile which could obliterate that future as we might conceive it, would be as fair game for ethnography, if it survived that Armageddon, as would be any other relics of our own civilization.

A future British Museum might well find traces of minis, maxis, jumbo-jets and Jehovah's Witnesses, all of equal grist to its perceptive mill – if such traces survived our self-destructive holocaust. To be sure, from where we stand at this present instant, the Hazda can be viewed simply as a tiny tribe of some 800 persons living in an area of about 1000 square miles to the east and west of Lake Eyasi in northern Tanzania. Yet, through the British Museum they emerge as such a timeless symbol of man's humanity and inhumanity to man as does our own terrifying selection of contemporary priorities.

The leaders of this world, at this minute, have at their disposal sufficient human energy, intelligence, technological resources and money, to endow, equip and staff hundreds of complete universities, farms, factories and their accompanying homes, to an extent which might conceivably transform totally the future of mankind: yet we seem to have chosen so far to devote this almost terrifying and yet temporary abundance of power over nature into putting satellites into orbit round the earth, and human beings on to the surface of the moon.

Pre-Columbian cultures of the Americas, Incas, Aztecs and Mayans, are repre-sented at the British Museum, simply but exquisitely by the turquoise mosaics from Mexico, which remind us of other vanished civilizations whose traces can

Bronze plaque by the Master of the Circled Cross, possibly the first of the plaque masters *(left)*

Bronze plaque by the Battle Master, showing a Benin warrior attacking a mounted Ibo, who has been seriously wounded across the chest *(right)*

still be found at Taxilla in north-west Pakistan and at Zimbabwe in Rhodesia.

An imaginative love of art for art's sake, as well as the crafts which make such art possible, penetrates to the heart of man's creativity in the exhibits of Palestinian Embroidery, Spinning and Weaving in Palestine, The Potter's Art in Africa, and the Raffles Gamelan, a great and ancient orchestra from Java which perhaps brought home for the first time to the Victorians that men and women beyond the ken of their civilization could love music and create it in a far greater profusion and complexity than those ancient Greeks with their lyres and lutes. The Gamelan was, and still is, the traditional and essential accompaniment to puppet-shows.

The essence of ethnography lies in the patient, persistent and systematic piecing together of scattered fragments of long-lost and often forgotten jigsaw puzzles of man's past cultural creations. What began as a motley collection of curios brought here by adventurers and explorers suddenly sprang to a marvellous significance when men of the imagination and superlative vision and sensibility of Sir Hans Sloane perceived a timeless order in an apparent chaos of assorted colourful junk. Unfortunately, not all the adventurers shared that feeling, or showed that mixture of forbearance and wonder which enables the exhibition to give so sparkling and yet so balanced a cross-section of history. Not only gadgets but guns paved the way of the explorers; and Hilaire Belloc, in his poetic inquiry into the real basis of the apparent moral and intellectual superiority of Western man over 'the wily Hottentot', summed it up in a sentence: 'We have got the Maxim gun and they have not'.

Much of the collection is the plunder of punitive military expeditions. The relics of the Benin tribe in the section on Divine Kingship in Africa are here as a result of war with the British. One attribute of divine kingship must be that a divine king can determine the destiny of mortal men: the Pope can still excommunicate, and thereby exclude a man from the Sacraments of his Church: but the Oba of the Benin tribe could and indeed did demand, as part of his divine authority, massive human sacrifices on a terrifying scale, as recently as within the last hundred years. Hence the punitive expedition in 1897 which led to a great massacre; and hence the vivid impact of the reconstruction of the royal palace, captured almost intact, and mounted as the heart and centre of the ethno-graphic exhibition.

'Nature is cruel; Man is sick of blood: nature and Man can never be fast friends.' So wrote Matthew Arnold; but man can thirst for blood until a particularly hideous bath in it sickens him; and nature will always contain cruelty as well as a wondrous beauty and spontaneous self-renewing creativeness. But man is part of nature, and nature's cruelty is man's as well. Man is the only creature who has perfected weapons for his own destruction as a major exercise in his own cultural development. And when the Benin thought to repulse the British, they relied not only on their spears and clubs against the guns to which they had no answer and which inevitably and indifferently massacred them: they

Tangaroa Upao Vahu, the creator and sea god of the Polynesians, creating the other gods, and mankind

Two male bronze heads of the early (left) and later phases of the Middle Period

also sent out their mysterious magicians to conjure up the help of those gods who were supposedly their King's allies in battle.

Unlike Old Testament tales of battles long ago when the Lord intervened on the side of Joshua at Jericho, or sustained the arm of the leader of his people so that a day could be prolonged for a battle to be won, while presumably the earth's rotation slowed by divine intervention for the sake of military advantage; unlike the Red Sea's parting to facilitate flight out of Egypt, the gods to whom the Benin magicians appealed in 1897 resembled more those Graeco-Roman divine warriors, Castor and Pollux, who were capricious in their response to similar appeals. On this occasion at least they did not come; and the Benin were utterly and completely overthrown; their leader fled, humiliated, but later gave himself up for lifelong exile at Calabar.

But should we become sickened by the mixture of awe, authority and bloody splendour implied in the sacrificial bronzes and plaques we can turn to the exhibits which show man's constant quest for his own origin, and its divine inspiration.

The Tribal Image: wooden figure sculpture of the world, has as one of its most striking pieces, the prize of a collection made early in the nineteenth century by the pioneer missionaries of the London Missionary Society to illustrate the errors of the heathen, although not without some admiration of their artistry. This supreme reminder of our ceaseless search for the meaning, origin and purpose of our life, is represented by Tangaroa Upao Vahu (which means 'Tangaroa up in the sky'), the creator and sea god of the Polynesians, in the act of creating gods and men. All over him, like warts or papillomata, are small images – hominids and homunculi. The back of the figure is detachable and the body hollow; and when it was given up to the missionaries, it was filled with

yet more small images of gods and men, which may well have been put there to absorb divine power.

In medieval Europe, ravaged by plague, famine and war, darkness seemed to have returned to cover the earth. Only the monasteries kept the historical records on which our school-learning is based. Therein, Christians believed that while Roman, Greek and even perhaps before them Egyptian cultures on the northern fringe of the African littoral, had been pagan but heroic, the actual events of Genesis, the creation of the world, of life, and of mankind, had preceded the birth of Christ by only 4000 or 5000 years. It seems now that they had underestimated the time span which preceded them at least a million times over; but they were still men like us, creatures who could look before and after. In those monasteries, almost the only survivors and preservers of cultural endeavour, hard work was done under rigid discipline, religious art flourished and even music could be heard. Unknown to them, there were caves in Europe as well as Africa and Asia, where drawings showed that men had lived and looked upon the world with a wondrous vision hundreds of thousands of years before them; but these were not yet discovered, scarcely even imagined.

The seven days of Genesis seemed real enough to them: more real than Caldwell's brilliant three-day construction, or the 5000 million years for which it stood. But one thing is certain, medieval Christians knew that life is short and art is long: they believed in the future, but at least as much in a life after death, as in the future of their successors, of which they could have no image at all. It is easy to understand how they could truly believe that the greatest sin of which man had originally been capable was the sin of discovering the fact of good and evil in the world; and thence the inescapable knowledge that he could make his choice. And yet if man had never discovered this, human choice would have been meaningless, and God, whatever or wherever he may be, would have had nothing even as exciting as the shadow puppets of Java for his creatures.

Man's art has always been a bridge between what Len Deighton has called our leaden lot and our golden potential. At the British Museum can be seen wonderful, terrible and beautiful fragments of both of these aspects of man's activity. From the first wheel, the first fire, the first weapon and the first pot to carry water, his art, his culture, his tradition, his aspirations, his fears and his defiant, desperate courage, have contributed to what ethnography selects for descriptive study. If indeed the proper study of mankind is man, then one marvellous place to start it is in the British Museum's ethnography exhibition.

Pair of carved wooden doors from the Palace at Ekere-Ekiti, eastern Yorubaland, carved by Olowe of Ise and representing the reception of the first British administrator, Captain Ambrose, by the Ogoga of Ikere about 1895

Chapter Twelve

Manuscripts

Asa Briggs

There are few professional historians in Britain – or post-graduate students working in universities on historical topics – who have not paid at least one visit to the Manuscripts Department of the British Museum. There are many historians, indeed, who go there as often as they can, armed with notebooks and a plentiful supply of sharp pencils. To them the British Museum, like the Public Record Office in Chancery Lane, is a workshop, and the noise of twentieth-century London is shut out as they return through their studies not only to historic London but to the whole of the lost world of the past.

The collections of the Manuscripts Department span twenty-three centuries and link our twentieth-century civilization with the world's first international library and museum in ancient Alexandria (founded by Ptolemy about 290 B.C. but destroyed in the seventh century). (Indeed, one precious manuscript of the Bible, the *Codex Alexandrinus*, as delicate as lace, made its way to the Museum after being presented by the Greek Patriarch to the King of England in the seventeenth century.) The century in which I am particularly interested, however, is the nineteenth, and I want to understand it and the people who lived in it rather than to escape into it. This, of course, was the century when the idea of the professional historian was born. There had been plenty of historians before then, not least in the ancient world and in the Middle Ages – men like Matthew Paris, the monk of St Albans, who died in 1259 and whose fascinating manuscript chronicles are preserved in the British Museum (1) – but history had never been thought of as a scholarly discipline in which people were engaged full-time, not only reading about history or teaching it but carrying out what came to be called 'original research'. During the nineteenth century some people approached history as a science, treating historical documents as the raw material which constituted their basic evidence. They collected information in the same spirit as Charles Darwin collected evidence about the world of nature. Above all else they wanted to dispel the legends and the myths which shrouded the past and at the same time to get behind the veil of propaganda – there has never been any shortage of this – to the real truth of what had actually happened. The best way of doing this seemed to be to get back to the original sources, to the kind of primary materials which are assembled in the Manuscripts Department and

1. Map of Great Britain by Matthew Paris; mid-thirteenth century
(Royal MS. 14, C. vii, f. 5b)

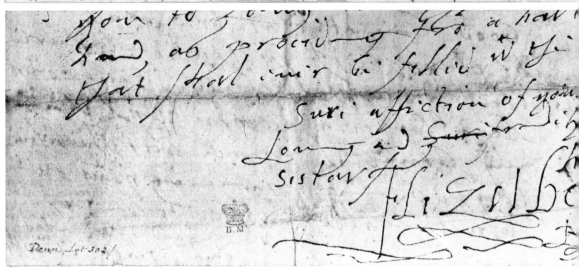

2. Letter written by Henry V in 1419, relating to prisoners taken at Agincourt (Cotton MS., Vespasian F, iii, f. 8) (*top*)

3. Letter from Elizabeth I to James VI of Scotland, dated 5 January 1603, two months before her death (Add. MS. 18738, f. 39) (*bottom*)

were being assembled in similar fashion in many other parts of Europe.

First, they had to guarantee the authenticity of the manuscripts, directing attention to the forgeries: this required detective work of a high order. Next they had to read and, if necessary translate, them before going on to interpret them, to evaluate their reliability and to assess their significance. Then they believed that they had a duty to publish them, making them freely available to scholars of all countries, so that they could be considered alongside other evidence. None of these tasks was easy, and difficulties often began with the actual reading of the documents. The way of forming letters has changed through the ages, and ex-perts in what we call 'palaeography' were needed to deal with complicated scripts, leading up eventually to the handwriting of our own times (2, 3 and 4, showing medieval, Elizabethan and Victorian scripts). Some of the old scripts are very beautiful, and the illustrations in what we call 'illuminated manuscripts' (6), written texts with pictures, sometimes of whole scenes, sometimes in the margins with signs and symbols, are revealing in themselves.

There can be few historians, however, who have not wished devoutly at times that the manuscripts they were studying, including not only those in the 'secretary hand' of the sixteenth and seventeenth centuries but those in the diverse and often highly idiosyncratic handwriting of nineteenth-century politicians, had been typed rather than written. But the first typewriters, like the first telephones, belong to the last decades of the nineteenth century. Their invention was one step in a continuing communications revolution which started with the invention of printing in the fifteenth century. We cannot understand the significance or use of manuscripts, which continue to be produced in larger and larger quantities even in an age of electric circuitry, unless we understand the problems of communicating as well as recording.

The study of historical sources does not in itself constitute history, and we now realize that there are far more historical sources – of a non-documentary kind – than the historians of the nineteenth century ever imagined. We can learn from landscapes and portraits as well as from manuscripts, from songs as well as from chronicles. Yet without the study of written sources there can be no history. It was during the nineteenth century that the Department of Manuscripts at the British Museum really came into its own. It had been one of the three original Departments of the Museum in the eighteenth century, and when the Museum

4. Conclusion of a letter from Charles Dickens to Miss Catherine Hogarth, written shortly before their marriage in 1836, while he was at work on *The Pickwick Papers* (Add. MS. 43689, f. 111b)

> *Friday September 11th 1795*
>
> ## Division 4
>
> It is with regret this Division reviews the loss of time which the London Corresponding Society has sustained from the ~~numerous~~ numerous motions which have been referred to the Divisions for altering its regulations;—a circumstance which, in the opinion of this Division, tends much to increase the business of the General Committee, as well as to defeat the object of the Society: inasmuch as the time of the Society is wasted in Cavils and disputes upon mere punctilios and questions of form when it might be employed to greater advantage in reading Political Books or discussing political questions; remedy this evil in future —
>
> It is moved that no motions that relate to the Constitution of Society be discussed more than twice in every six Months, and that the Executive Committee do appoint stated times for that purpose. —
>
> ffor it 21
> ag.st it 4
>
> Peter Campbell Chairman
> F. Follett Secretary

5. Extract from the papers of the London Corresponding Society (Add. MS 27813, f. 136)

first opened its doors in 1753 it already possessed as many as 15,000 manuscript volumes, many of them collected, some of them plundered, by Sir Robert Cotton, a member of the Elizabethan Society of Antiquaries, who still deserves to be remembered for his pioneering enterprise. The Manuscripts Department now holds 75,000 volumes and about 100,000 charters. Yet we must be careful about quantitative estimates. A volume may consist of a single text or a score of letters. It was during the nineteenth-century Keepership of Sir Frederic Madden, who took over his post in 1837, the year when Queen Victoria came to the throne, and stayed there until 1866, that some of the biggest collections of manuscripts were built up, a number of them dealing with countries like Italy and Spain as well as Britain. Madden spent sums of up to £3000 a year on manuscripts. This sum does not sound very substantial these days, yet it would require up to £100,000 a year today to follow the same kind of purchasing policy as that of Madden, assuming impossibly that the same kinds of materials were available. Again we must be careful of statistics. Many manuscripts are priceless, because they are unique. It is sometimes said that libraries fall into two categories – those of first resort and those of last resort – you go to those of last resort if you cannot

6. Christmas scenes from the De Lisle Psalter, illuminated in England c. 1300–20 (Arundel MS. 83 II, f. 124)

Gloria in Excelsis Deo

find your books somewhere else: the Manuscripts Department of the Museum, however, holds for the most part a collection of *only* resort. You go there, or there is nowhere else where you can go.

The proportion of the total British Museum purchasing grant spent on buying manuscripts fell in the twentieth century, but it has more than doubled again during the last three years. Moreover, for every manuscript bought – and some like the *Codex Sinaiticus*, an early Bible bought from the Soviet Union for £100,000 in 1933, have been very expensive – several have been given. Indeed, it is almost as prestigious to have a collection of your manuscripts in the British Museum as to have your statue in Westminster Abbey.

Not that a historian is particularly worried about prestige. He is interested in what the manuscripts actually say, and sometimes the manuscripts of minor historical personalities may provide more vital evidence than those of the people whose names were once household words. When I go back to the Museum myself, the manuscripts, which interest me most as a nineteenth-century historian include not only the Peel and Gladstone papers, remarkably large and rich collections, but the equally impressive collection of Radical papers kept by Francis Place, the London tailor, which bring back to life, though always

7. Extract from Gladstone's notes for a Cabinet Meeting, 1869 (Add. MS. 44637, f. 102)

through Francis Place's own eyes, the society and politics of Radical London in the early decades of the nineteenth century. If Place had not collected these papers, they would almost certainly have disappeared. The Place Collection includes the Minute Books and Letters Books of the London Corresponding Society (5), which under the direction of its brave and energetic founder, the shoe-maker, Thomas Hardy, gathered together the threads of London popular Radicalism in the stormy decade of the 1790s. The historian owes much to Francis Place, even if at times he becomes exasperated with his limitations, because Place, with no formal education, was a born archivist. 'I cannot, like many other men,' he once wrote, 'go to a tavern. I hate taverns and tavern company. I cannot drink. I cannot for any time consent to converse with fools.' We can be thankful for these qualities, and also for the fact that though he would not willingly converse with fools, he was prepared to keep in his collection papers written by people whom he believed to be the biggest fools in the land. Like Matthew Paris centuries before him, he liked to feel that he was 'in the know', and like Paris also, he had a good eye for significant detail.

The Gladstone Papers, which are assembled in no fewer than 750 volumes, were presented to the British Museum by Gladstone's relatives in 1930. Hitherto

8. Extract from Jonathan Swift's *Journal to Stella*, 1712 (Add. MS. 4804, f. 58)

9. The opening lines of 'Kubla Khan' by Samuel Taylor Coleridge, composed in 1797 and first published in 1816 (Add. MS. 50847)

they had been kept in an annexe to Gladstone's library in Hawarden Castle. The Papers cover every conceivable kind of subject (7), for Gladstone's range of interests was far wider than that of most twentieth-century – and, for that matter, nineteenth-century – Prime Ministers. As one of his biographers has written, Gladstone was convinced that God would call him personally to account for his every thought, word and deed, and, not surprisingly in consequence, he preserved over a quarter of a million pieces of paper. This is not quite the end of the story, however. A historian anxious to tell the truth about Gladstone – as a person and as a major figure in politics – must behave in exactly the same way as a historian anxious to tell the truth about anybody or anything else. He must trace every aspect of Gladstone's career from schoolboy to Tory politician and from Tory politician to Liberal statesman, the 'Grand Old Man'. He must also look to see what papers are *not* to be found in the Manuscripts Department as well as at those which are. Among the crucial documents missing from the British Museum is a private journal kept by Gladstone in forty volumes. He first began to keep it in 1825 when he was only sixteen years old. Since 1928 the journal has been kept in the Library of the Archbishop of Canterbury, Lambeth Palace, where it was thought by his relatives to be especially safe. Now, at last, it is being published. And to complete the Gladstone story, a bundle of extremely important papers, buried away in the office of quite dull and stupid for things to go on in the common way.

So she set to work, and very soon finished off the cake.

*   *   *   *   *

"Curiouser and curiouser!" cried Alice, (she was so surprised that she quite forgot how to speak good English,) "now I'm opening out like the largest telescope that ever was! Goodbye, feet!" (for when she looked down at her feet, they seemed almost out of sight, they were getting so far off,) "oh, my poor little feet, I wonder who will put on your shoes and stockings for you now, dears? I'm sure I can't! I shall be a great deal too far off to bother myself about you: you must manage the best way you can — but I must be kind to them", thought Alice, "or perhaps they won't walk the way I want to go! Let me see: I'll give them a new pair of boots every Christmas."

And she went on planning to herself how she would manage it

10. Extract from Lewis Carroll's original manuscript of *Alice's Adventures Under Ground*, given as a Christmas present to Alice Liddell in 1864 and published in 1865 as *Alice's Adventures in Wonderland* (Add. MS. 46700, f. 7)

11. Part of the Concerto in A for piano, Adagio in D, by Beethoven, from the Kafka sketch-book which contains his autograph drafts of various compositions (Add. MS. 29801, f. 154b)

Macmillans, the publishers, has recently been discovered. The papers were studied by John Morley, Gladstone's disciple and first outstanding biographer, and then put on one side because they were exceptionally secret and covered critical episodes in Gladstone's long political life. They have now, at last, been deposited in the British Museum. The historian can illustrate almost every problem of historical research from questions arising out of the Gladstone Papers which were in the hands of the same knowledgeable cataloguer, Arthur Tilney Bassett, before and after they were moved from Hawarden to London. The questions range from the future of Ireland or the relations between Church and State to why General Gordon was sent to Khartoum and why he perished there.

To catalogue manuscripts – a protracted, at times a heartbreaking task,

12. The Articles of the Barons: demands accepted by King John at Runnymede in June 1215 as a basis for Magna Carta (Add. MS. 4838)

rather like the labours of Hercules – and to assist historians and answer inquiries from outside, the Manuscripts Department employs a sizeable staff – one Keeper, three Deputy Keepers, two Assistant Keepers and seven Research Assistants. In terms of numbers of staff, therefore, the Department is the second largest in the Museum. It includes a special Sub-Department of Modern Historical Papers, created in 1948 to deal with the vast mass of nineteenth- and twentieth-century material which was threatening to swamp the whole Department.

One of the effects of the great expansion of university research studies in history in recent years has been the subjection of the Department as a whole and the Modern Sub-Department in particular to immense pressures. Before the Second World War there was a steady attendance record of 11,000 to 12,000 attendances a year, but by 1970 the attendance had risen to over 20,000: it has been continuing to rise ever since. There has also been as great an increase in the number of letters received from the outside public, itself a measure, doubtless, of the rise in the level of general education. The Students' Room at the Museum has spaces for some sixty readers and the turnover frequently exceeds eighty a day. Often the 'Full House' sign has to be displayed. Manuscripts are normally supplied within ten minutes of asking, a very speedy form of service. And although most of the manuscripts predate the use of telephones and typewriters – and many, of course, predate by centuries the invention of printing – modern technology is now at the disposal of the historian. There are microfilm-readers in the Department and the number of photocopies made of manuscripts has more than doubled during the last ten years.

The application of computer techniques to the cataloguing and indexing of manuscripts is still in its infancy, but the day will certainly come when the historian will have the chance not only of taking advantage of the new technology in dealing with old manuscripts but of studying audio-visual evidence – in recordings and films, the latter of immense value, particularly perhaps to the social historian – to supplement what he can find out from his piles of paper. From papyrus to parchment and from parchment to paper will be followed by from paper to celluloid and the other synthetic materials. Historical evidence will certainly change: so, too, will historical method. It is no longer fanciful to contemplate historians studying manuscripts not in the Students' Room but in distant parts of the world with new forms of telecommunication providing the medium.

All this is in the future. When I work at the Museum as a modern historian in the fleeting present, I am always well aware that I am handling precious materials which constitute only a small part – and those visitors to the Department who are not professional historians may say not even the most interesting

13. The Lindisfarne Gospels: decorative 'carpet' page preceding St Mark's Gospel in the codex written and illuminated *c.* 698 in honour of St Cuthbert (Cotton MS., Nero D., iv, f. 94b)

14. Letter of Edmund Clere, Bailiff of the Duchy of Lancaster, to his cousin John Paston I, 1455 (Add. MS. 43488, f. 21)

part – of the possessions in the hands of the Keeper of Manuscripts. Alongside those of its written manuscripts which are of importance in political and social history, the Department also holds texts of poems and plays, all of which require – and receive – just as close critical scrutiny as any letter from a politician or a memorandum prepared for a Cabinet. The original copy of Jonathan Swift's *Journal to Stella* (8) was presented to the Manuscripts Department as early as 1766. It is only one of many literary treasures which take the reader back to Pindar or Sappho or Coleridge's *Kubla Khan* (9) and on to the modern poet W. H. Auden and beyond. It is fascinating to examine such a nineteenth-century manuscript as Lewis Carroll's *Alice's Adventures Under Ground* (10), the author's first draft (with his own illustrations) of *Alice's Adventures in Wonderland*, which was published in 1865. This and Carroll's other books remain at least as interesting to adults as they are to children: they certainly link up Oxford, the Oxford of the sweet dreaming spires, as depicted in Buckler's drawings, and wonderland, with mathematics serving as a spur both to the controlled imagination and to the wildest fantasy. In the twenty-first century, students will be able

15. 'Summer is icumen in', a part-song written in the mid-thirteenth century, probably at Reading Abbey (Harley MS. 978, f. 11b)

to go to the Manuscripts Department to study autographed manuscripts of most contemporary English poets, for since 1962 the Museum and the Arts Council have been joint sponsors of a collection of representative manuscripts. An exhibition was held in 1967 of some of the treasures already acquired by that date. Another interesting recent acquisition was 773 volumes of plays from the office of the Lord Chamberlain. A wise historian of the future should be able to make use of these as a stimulating, if difficult, source.

Nor is literature the only supplement to history. Alongside its written materials, historical and literary, the Manuscripts Department also collects papyri, manuscript maps, some of them extremely beautiful, revealing how our ancestors thought and felt about the world and its exploration, manuscript music, including some of the great music of all nations (11), seal impressions and casts, a subject for the expert, who can learn as much from them as other experts from handwriting, and brass rubbings, which provide a hobby for enthusiasts from many countries. It does not need an expert to appreciate the beauty or the cultural significance of many of these items. As the great Victorian novelist, George Eliot, wrote in 1855, 'for the common eye there is nothing to compare with the stupendous relics of the British Museum'. Thirty-five years later an American writer noted that the Museum 'guards its jewels jealously': in his opinion the Manuscripts Department was one of the wonders of London, if not of the world.

Interested though I am in the great jewels from all parts of the world, including the ancient world, I must confess that, like every other British visitor to the Museum, I am particularly interested in those jewels which have a special place in our own national heritage. This is, after all, the British Museum, and it has a special responsibility to bring our national past to life, for the benefit not just of specialized historians but for everybody. I would not claim to be an authority on Magna Carta, about which many scholarly books and articles have been written, but my eyes always turn to Magna Carta in the permanent exhibition which the Department always keeps on display (12). Magna Carta is as much of a jewel as the Crown Jewels in the Tower of London. The purpose of the original Great Charter in 1215 was to guarantee the feudal rights of the great barons and to ensure that the King did not encroach on their privileges, but in later centuries the Charter came to be thought of as a symbol of the supremacy of law over the King, part of the Bills of the Constitution. Like many historical documents of lesser importance, Magna Carta has meant different things to different generations. But to most visitors it is as much the idea of seeing Magna Carta which counts – and, not least King John's seal – as of pondering on its changing meanings. It seems right and proper that it should be kept in the heart of twentieth-century London, and it is.

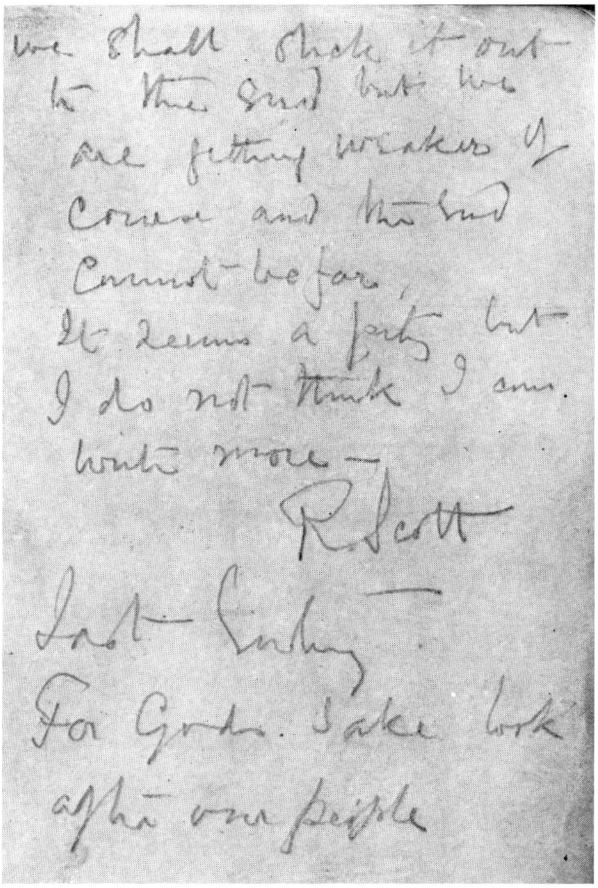

We shall stick it out
to the end but we
are getting weaker of
course and the end
cannot be far,
It seems a pity but
I do not think I can
write more —
R. Scott
Last entry.
For God's sake look
after our people

16. The final entry in Captain Scott's Antarctic Diary, 29 March 1912 (Add. MS. 51035)

There is no other national treasure which commands quite as much general attention, but few visitors to the Manuscripts Department would want to miss the seventh-century Lindisfarne Gospels (13), where the oldest prose translation into English of the Gospels was added to the text in the tenth century. The translation is believed to have been made by a priest called Aldred, who was Bishop of Durham in about A.D. 950, and he wrote his translation between the lines of his Latin Vulgate Bible. The earliest complete translation of the Bible was made by John Wycliffe in the fourteenth century, still before the age of printing. To me these early English Bibles are more immediately interesting than the great *Codex Sinaiticus* which is a key document in the history of Christianity. They belong to our developing national culture, a culture which, as the turbulent career of Wycliffe showed, always had a place for discontent and protest as well as for order and authority. I like to go back, too, to the Paston Letters, which I first heard about at school (14). This is a collection, unique in its range and detail, of the personal and business correspondence of the Paston family in Norfolk during the fifteenth century: it is an indispensable collection for those interested in the customs and history of the period. An even earlier national treasure is the first version, way back in the thirteenth century, of the Old English song 'Sumer is icumen in' (15) which in its way is as interesting as the universal music of Mozart and Beethoven to which I have already paid homage. As I move down the centuries I am glad that the Manuscripts Department provides a home for such other well-known pieces in English History as Nelson's letters to Lady Hamilton or from the twentieth century itself Captain Scott's Antarctic Diary (16) with its unforgettable entry for 29 March 1912: 'It seems a pity but I do not think I can write more'; and its haunting final entry: 'For God's sake look after our people.'

In the last resort, the Manuscripts Department is for 'our people'. It serves from one generation to another as a collective memory for the nation as well as a treasure-house for mankind.

Chapter Thirteen

Coins and Medals

John Hale

The unusual thing about coin-collecting is that it involves spending a version of the very thing you are buying. To separate the sense of collecting from merely acquiring for immediate gain requires a particularly strong feeling of 'distance' between the object in your cabinet and the object in your pocket. This was provided by the cult of antiquity which affected so many educated men in Renaissance Italy. They were able to make a radical distinction between the ducats and florins they spent, and the aurei, denarii and sestertii they collected. Lorenzo the Magnificent, for example, left a collection of more than 3200 coins, about a third of which came from a collection formed by a pope, Paul II.

England profited from Italian experience. The first of the many collections acquired by the British Museum was that of Sir Robert Cotton, who died in 1631. It came to the Museum in 1753 and since then, by purchase, but mostly by gift and bequest, London's collection of coins and medals has accumulated to a range, interest and quality that can only be rivalled by Paris and Berlin. The range stretches in time from the first true coins of *c.* 700 B.C. to the latest drab offerings of the Royal Mint, and in space from London to Tokyo and Canberra.

There are nearly three-quarters of a million coins and hundreds of thousands of medals. Visitors' and students' interest in the Department spans the whole spectrum of historical, social, economic and iconographical inquiry and draws on the Museum's role in the detection of forgeries as well as its role in providing the scholarly base-line from which collectors, dealers and other museums plan their acquisitions. But for the moment let us concentrate on the art of making coins and medals which developed in two extraordinary spurts; the first in the ancient Greek world, the second in Renaissance Italy.

One of the world's greatest labour-saving devices, coinage was invented some 2700 years ago. It was not, of course, the earliest form of payment. Men had been exchanging goods by barter for thousands of years before the first coin was struck, and in the most economically sophisticated part of the world, in the lands round the eastern Mediterranean, the precious metals, gold, silver and bronze had been used for centuries to pay taxes, tribute and the wages of mercenary soldiers, to make offerings to the gods or to purchase animals. But

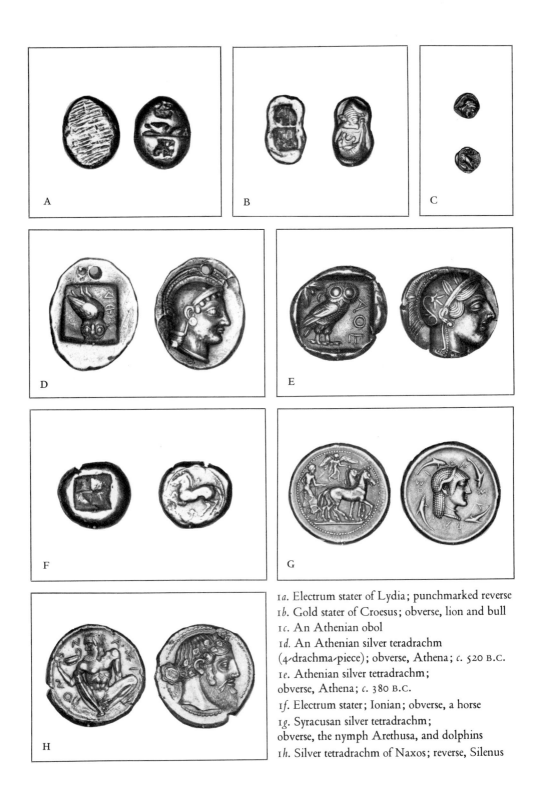

1*a*. Electrum stater of Lydia; punchmarked reverse
1*b*. Gold stater of Croesus; obverse, lion and bull
1*c*. An Athenian obol
1*d*. An Athenian silver teradrachm
(4-drachma-piece); obverse, Athena; *c.* 520 B.C.
1*e*. Athenian silver tetradrachm;
obverse, Athena; *c.* 380 B.C.
1*f*. Electrum stater; Ionian; obverse, a horse
1*g*. Syracusan silver tetradrachm;
obverse, the nymph Arethusa, and dolphins
1*h*. Silver tetradrachm of Naxos; reverse, Silenus

though metal used for such purposes might reasonably be called 'cash' or 'currency', its shape and size was unfixed and its value varied from place to place. The first step towards coin was taken when purchasing power was deliberately related to weight, when so much bronze, say, or gold was generally understood to be the equivalent in cash of a cow. Some of the pre-coin currency was in fact shaped like a cow's hide – great planks of bronze nearly a yard long and weighing sixty or so pounds. This agreed relationship between a certain weight of metal and a basic commodity turned currency into money, but it was still something like a thousand years before a stamp was put on the metal, thus turning it into a coin.

A coin is a readily portable piece of metal bearing a stamp which identifies its place of origin and value. For the value, or the purchasing power of a coin, unlike that of a piece of metal used as money, does not have to be the exact equivalent of an unstamped, or un-coined piece of metal of the same size and weight. In addition to its intrinsic value (its worth when melted down as bullion) it acquires a symbolic value, greater or less than the value of bullion according to the degree of confidence between the Government striking the coins and the people using them. Thus, when coinage was introduced, mankind not only obtained a labour-saving device but became involved in monetary policy and the deliberate manipulation of coin value with all the attendant dangers – debasement, slumps, inflations – with which we have become so familiar.

Coin represents an intellectualization of money and it is appropriate that it was invented in Greek-dominated Lydia, in Asia Minor. The oldest coin in the Department of Coins and Medals' collection is probably one of the earliest of all true coins, a Lydian stater with three punch-marks on the reverse – the upper side of an ingot when it was struck. The obverse – the lower side, which lies against the face of the anvil – has an apparently aimless pattern of scratches on it and the whole coin resembles a small oval pebble (1a). But from this start with the *idea* of a coin, the progress towards the *form* of a coin, instantly recognizable in modern terms, was amazingly swift. Another very early specimen, also from Lydia, not only has the figure of a crouching lion on its obverse, made by a die fixed in the anvil, but marks made by the punches driving the hot ingots against the anvil themselves carry decorative motifs; the one most clearly visible on the Museum's specimen represents a clear, if rudimentary, stag's head. It is not yet round. For some time, indeed, coins could be irregular or positively bean-shaped, like the gold stater struck by King Croesus – the Rich – of Sardis (1b). This coin, with its bull and lion confronting one another on the obverse, represents a third stage taken in Lydia towards the coinage of the future, for Croesus began the idea of strict bimetallism by making his gold stater exactly twenty times the value of the silver stater, so that for the first time it was possible to make change in a straightforward manner.

Gold, silver and electrum (a natural alloy of gold and silver) were the metals most used in coinage for several centuries. Thus all coins were of a considerable purchasing power, used far less in the market-place than for the payment of taxes or wages (the gold stater was a month's wages for a mercenary soldier) or to hoard – often in a buried pot – against a time of need. The demand for small change was only gratified from the fifth century, and then, either because of the expense of minting large bronze coins of low value or of the difficulty of relating the purchasing power of bronze to silver, small change was made of silver. And small change, in the most literal sense, it was (1c). The pocket-less Greeks carried obols in their mouths when they went marketing and presumably became adept at not swallowing them. Even the smallest silver coin, the Athenian half obol, had roughly the purchasing power of a fifty new penny piece today, so daily transactions must still have relied chiefly on barter. From the fourth century B.C., bronze small change began to be used, but it is doubtful even then whether it could serve for purchases worth less than twenty-five of our new pennies.

Early Greek coins, then, changed hands far less frequently than our own coins do; they were worth more, they were used less casually, and there was more time to finger and to look at them. It is not surprising that from a remarkably short time after their introduction coins not only came to look like works of art but were deliberately created as works of art. And it is this aspect, perhaps, even more than the sense of contact with the past they can give or the historical information they can provide, that motivates most collectors.

Though coins do not necessarily reflect stylistic changes that occur in painting and sculpture, they seldom remain unaffected for long periods. Thus the Athenian was one of the more conservative of Greek coinages, but this taut and nervous Athena (1d) superbly encapsulates much that is essential to our response to the Archaic Greek art of about 500 B.C., while the later version of the goddess (1e) perfectly expressed the move towards a calm, almost sensuous gravity that marks the art of about 380 B.C. as a whole. The tendency for the reverse of a coin to become the carrier not merely of the punch-mark which guaranteed its value but of artistic designs, was promoted by the example of engraved seals and the existence of a highly trained core of die-cutters who made both these and dies made to stamp decoration into, say, jewellery. The early Lydian lion clearly derives from a seal, and his rectangular border is at odds with the oval shape of the coin. Before long, however, design became completely adapted to the shape of the coin, whether the design was 'full', in the sense of filling the circular field, or 'open' in the sense of depending chiefly on the

2*a*. Athenian silver tetradrachm; obverse, owl

2*b*. Silver stater of Aegina; obverse, turtle

2*c*. Silver stater of Aegina struck some 300 years later

2*d*. Silver tetradrachm of Catana, signed; obverse, Apollo

2*e*. Silver tetradrachm of Egypt; obverse, Alexander the Great as conqueror (elephant skin) and god (ram's horn of Ammon)

2*f*. Silver tetradrachm of Pontus; obverse, Mithradates III

2*g*. Gold stater showing head of Mithradates III

2*h*. Bronze sestertius; oberse, bust of the Emperor Galba

balance between the decorative motif itself and the border. A very early example
of 'full' design is the galloping horse on the Ionian stater (1*f*). The skill with
which the dolphins are placed between the stern head of the nymph Arethusa
and the edge of the coin on the rather later Syracusan tetradrachm (1*g*) of
'open' design represents a vivacity and assurance of approach that has seldom
been surpassed in the 2500 years since the coin was struck. The letters are somewhat randomly placed, but the problem of relating letters to image and to border
has been solved by the time we reach the brilliantly designed Silenus from
Naxos (1*h*), and we have still only reached about 460 B.C.

Early coins of the Greek world contain, in fact, very little lettering. Many
have none at all. Nor was it customary to mark the value on coins except for
the clumsily designed bronze small change. Thus the die-engraver usually had
plenty of surface to play with, and it is the image's possibility of contact with the
edge, rather than with a continuous inscription, that contributed to their satisfactory massiveness – as in so many of the 'eagle' staters of Elis, or to their springy
exuberance – as with the 'hares' of Sicily. The Athenian owl owes much of his
charm to his not being caged by words (2*a*).

Obverses commonly bore the image of an animal associated with the town
minting the coins. Hence the leather-backed turtle which represented Aegina
and swam along the trade-routes of the Mediterranean and Asia Minor. The fact
that towns commonly chose creatures that were a commonplace of the local
scene (whether for their own sake, as the Aeginan turtle or the crab of Agrigento,
or as personifications of protecting deities, such as the eagle for Jove, or a cow
for Io) meant that the style was constantly refreshed by actual observation. Look
at the difference between two turtles (2*b* and *c*) separated by some 300 years.
And that coins were treated deliberately as works of art, responsive to changes
of style in the other arts, is clear not only from their quality but from their being
frequently signed by the die-engraver.

The personality of the engraver of the Apollo series of Catanian tetradrachms,
c. 400 B.C. (2*d*) has much to do with putting these among the most beautiful
coins ever produced. Here Apollo is more god than man. The central Greek
world was, indeed, reluctant to allow the faces of ordinary mortals to appear on
their coins. The move towards realistic portraiture moved slowly through
representations of men as gods – as in the late fourth-century coins which show
Alexander the Great deified, wearing the horns of Ammon (2*e*). By 200 B.C.,
however, the straightforward portrait of a ruler was becoming fairly common.
It was an approach that produced works of naturalistic genius, like the sad-
dened figure of Mithradates III (2*f*). But numismatic portraiture was too sharply
affected by political aims to reflect the other contemporary arts consistently.
This tired servant of his people was succeeded a century later by another

3. Pisanello; diverse, portrait of Don Iñigo de'Avalos   4. Reverse of number 3

Mithradates, Mithradates VI, who wanted to appear as their inspired master, the Golden Boy – it is a gold coin – of Kings (2*g*).

It was the coins of Rome and, above all, of the Roman emperors, that were most easily available and had the strongest appeal to the collectors of Renais-sance Italy. Here were the likenesses of their revered ancestors together with inscriptions recording their fame. The most impressive influence of this interest in ancient Roman money was not so much on Renaissance coins, however, as on almost new art form, the medal. In the first place there was a formal in-fluence on the development of the medal which derived from the profile portrait the nature of the inscription and the type of lettering (2*h*). There was also a functional influence. The Romans used coinage much more frankly for propa-ganda purposes than did the Greeks, glorifying leadership, commemorating battles and political *coups*, celebrating victories. Nero, for instance, celebrated the end of the Parthian War in A.D. 63 by striking a sestertius showing his head on one side and on the other the Temple of Janus with its doors closed, symbol of the peace 'by land and sea' which the Emperor had brought to the whole Empire. This sort of self-glorifying propaganda was taken up by the Renais-sance medal-makers at a time when coins were little used to convey a 'message'; indeed, the best-trusted coins, like the Florentine florin or the Venetian ducat, still retained in the fifteenth century the form merchants had relied on when they were first issued two centuries before.

5. Matteo de' Pasti;
obverse, portrait of
Isotta degli Atti

6. Reverse of number 5

Like the coin, the medal came to artistic maturity within a surprisingly short time after its introduction – in mid-fifteenth-century Italy. This was partly, of course, because the Roman coin was already there to suggest its form: the round shape, different designs on obverse and reverse, the portrait bust, the inscription running round the edge. The greatest functional difference between the medal and the coin was that a medal could not be used as money. The chief formal differences were that commonly its size was much larger than that of a coin and that it was generally made of bronze or lead not, as was the case of the most carefully designed coins, of gold or silver.

Its purpose was above all commemorative. The portrait medal was a way of circulating a likeness to a selected few – a lover, friends, a circle of statesmen. More portable than a painting, it anticipated the purpose of the miniature and was, indeed, frequently worn round the neck. Unlike the miniature, however, it could be reproduced. Attached to a wall, or lying on a table, it played something like the role of the portrait photograph today, with the distinction that the medal carried with it a greater sense of dignity, derived from its association with the coinage of ancient Rome, and bore on its reverse a design that purported to convey the 'essence', as it were, of the person portrayed. Thanks to these last two factors the Renaissance medal had a talismanic force that no other form of portraiture, before or since, has attained.

Taking together a number of traits fairly common to educated and influential men in the fifteenth century: passionate admiration for the men and the

7. Reverse of Niccolò Fiorentino's medal of Giovanna Albizzi

8. Giovanna Maria Pomedelli; reverse of medal of Elisabetta da Vicenza

9. Obverse of number 8 showing portrait of Elisabetta da Vicenza

artefacts of ancient Rome, stress on individual character, desire for earthly fame and a penchant for summing-up temperament in symbols and images, it is easy to understand how quickly the fashion for commissioning medals spread. But it also becomes all the more remarkable that one man, Pisanello, was chiefly responsible for originating the idea. The precedents before he began to cast medals in 1438-9 had been few, and excessively coin-like. Within ten years he had established the over-all form the medal was to retain throughout its existence and set an example of artistic achievement that has seldom been reached and never surpassed.

The only possible fault in his medal of Don Iñigo de'Avalos (3) is that it is almost too much like a painting; we want to know the colour of his hat and his eyes. But, though in fact a painter first and foremost, Pisanello seldom mis-judged the special limitations – and gains – of working from wax model to bronze casting; combining mass and detail, balancing image and inscription with amazing sureness. And in line with the proud self-consciousness that made men commission medals, he signed his name in such a way as to make it as important a part of the design of the reverse as was Don Iñigo's emblem itself: earth, sea and heavens forming a single sphere, as in Homer's description of Achilles' shield (4).

Before Pisanello's short career as a medallist was over, others were producing work almost as fine. In 1446, for example, Matteo de' Pasti celebrated Sigis-mondo Malatesta of Rimini's love for his mistress Isotta (5) by striking two medals. The reverses contradict any suggestion that Sigismondo's passion was a sign of weakness. Though married, he firmly staked his claim to Isotta by having Pasti put the Malatesta emblem of the elephant – for irresistible strength – on the reverse of her medal (6), and the citadel which he was then remodelling on the reverse of his.

10. Sperandio; reverse of medal
of Cardinal Francesco Gonzaga

11. Obverse of number 10
showing portrait of Cardinal
Francesco Gonzaga

Uncharacteristically, Florentines were not among the pioneers of the medal, but by the 1480s Niccolò Fiorentino was producing there some of the most relaxed-looking and successful medals of the Renaissance. Inside her ring of words, Giovanna Albizzi looks unassuming if intelligent. It is the reverse (7) that takes us into the air of cerebral flirtatiousness that educated women of her class breathed, with its intricate Neoplatonic debates about the nature of love; indeed, Pico della Mirandola himself had this reverse – based on an ancient statuary group – on a medal Niccolò did for him, but with an inscription that labelled the figures in a different way. Such a reverse, so easily graceful and so straightforwardly tactile, was none the less for contemporaries a point of entry into a highly esoteric world of philosophical discourse.

Part of the appeal of the medal was that to give one was not only to give an external likeness, but a clue to the donor's inner life: clues in a code that is often difficult and sometimes impossible to crack. What does this stick hitting a donkey, this axe stuck in a branch, this hammer hovering in the air (8) tell us of Elisabetta of Vicenza, whose portrait is on the obverse (9)? What is the significance of these two sets of armour, bow and quiver, one lying on the ground, one in the sky (10)? And what is that lynx, if it is a lynx, looking at, and why? What do we learn about Cardinal Francesco Gonzaga, whose medal this is (11)? The Gonzaga reverse, by Sperandio of Mantua (the Gonzaga city) is somewhat clumsy. In total contrast, both in message and quality, is another

12. A medal by Sperandio of Mantua

13. Lodovico Brognolo

of Sperandio's reverses (12). Nothing could be less recondite than the praying hands and the inscription 'My trust is in God', and this medal of the friar Lodovico Brognolo looks forward to the simple but dramatic effects for which the best medallists search today (13).

The occasion for commissioning a medal was frequently personal: a marriage, a death or simply the request of friends. Architectural projects were also cele- brated by medals showing the patron on one side and the building on the other. These had an additional, nearly magical role. The ancient custom of striking medals to bury in the foundation of palaces, temples and fortresses had been revived; they were to serve, as it were, as guardian spirits of the place. But political motives came to play an increasingly important part. In 1480 Lorenzo the Magnificent, negotiating with the Sultan Mohammad II to aid Florence by creating an armed diversion in southern Italy, commissioned his favourite sculptor, Bertoldo, to cast a medal to be sent to Mohammed and, very probably, to circulate among the supporters of Medicean policies. Bertoldo had already worked for Lorenzo, designing in 1478 a medal to celebrate his escape from assassins' daggers during the Pazzi plot to murder him at High Mass in the Cathedral, and their partnership was an important initial step in the medal's long career as an instrument of propaganda. His latest medal had the Sultan's head on the obverse (14) while on the reverse (15) Mars led a chariot on which

14. Obverse of number 15 showing portrait of Mohammed II

15. Bertoldo di Giovanni; reverse of medal of Mohammed II

16. Obverse of number 17 showing portrait of Alfonso, Duke of Calabria
17. Andrea Guacialoti; reverse of medal of Alfonso, Duke of Calabria

rode Victory holding a rope that secured three nude females symbolizing the Sultan's conquests in Greece, Asia and Trebizond. This Tamerlane-like concept is strengthened by the Neptune facing a figure representing the earth, an image inviting Mohammed to extend his conquests across the sea. And he did. In that year a large Turkish expeditionary force occupied the Italian Adriatic port of Otranto. After a year of terror they were defeated by the Duke of Calabria who thereupon commissioned from Andrea Guacialoti a medal which has the appearance, at least, of an answer to Bertoldo's message. On the obverse is a portrait of the Duke (16). The reverse (17) shows him riding aloft in a triumphal car preceded by troops who herd the remains of the Turkish army back to captivity in Otranto.

The success of the medal as a work of art depended on its being able to avoid on the one hand looking too much like money and on the other too much like a plaque, or miniature relief sculpture. The cult of antiquity could lead the medals to look dangerously like a large Roman coin: the work of the late fifteenth-century 'Lysippus Junior' (his real name is not known) reflects this tendency and it was accentuated by the gradual – though never total – replacement of the cast by the struck medal, a process which allowed less delicacy, hardened outlines and did not allow such deep relief. The danger of moving too near to the plaque was inherent in the use of the illustrative reverse. Some of Pisanello's – such as his marvellous depiction of two horsemen, one moving across the plain of the relief, the other moving directly away from it – are only saved from being round relief sculptures by their inscriptions. Some fifty years later even the inscription cannot save the reverse (18) of Matteo Olivieri's

18. Matteo Olivieri; reverse of medal of Altobello Averoldo showing 'truth unveiled'

medal of Altobello Averoldo from being a piece of sculpture rather than one side of a medal. A few years later, on a medal of Pietro Bembo, once attributed to Benvenuto Cellini, lettering has disappeared altogether, making the reverse resemble a large and beautiful button. The last step came later again in the sixteenth century with the works of men like Bombarda who gave up the reverse altogether and produced immensely elegant hollow-cast figures on a wafer-thin background (19). Without weight or reverse, the medal, after rather more than a century since Pisanello 'inherited' it, had become a bronze minia-ture. This is a personal, possibly an obsessively purist view. But if none of the tens of thousands of later medals in the Museum's collection rivals those of the Renaissance, they offer a lively, at times almost a monthly commentary on historical events whether commemorating individuals, treaties or battles. At times a whole campaign was mapped on their reverses.

It is a long road from Pisanello's Iñigo de'Avalos to the military 'gong' of today, but the Museum possesses nearly every milestone along the route, as it does for the far longer road from the Lydian stater to our present coinage. And those who wish to look to precedent in order to reform our present lacklustrely

19. A medal by Bombarda showing a portrait of his wife, Leonora Cambi

designed money could turn to another immense branch of the collection to which I have not yet referred: the multitudinous tokens used as substitutes for coins of the realm such as those handed out by employers in the labour-swamped towns of the Industrial Revolution. These factory tokens did not masquerade as precious metal and they took their imagery from the needs of the day, the mining of coal and the spinning of cotton, not from a flimsy parody of its heraldic nostalgia.

Departments of the Museum
and Biographical Notes

Departments of the Museum

Printed Books

The Department of Printed Books is based on the library of Sir Hans Sloane, which, at his death in 1753, consisted of some 50,000 volumes of printed books and manuscripts. To this was added in 1757 the old Royal Library of the Kings of England, a magnificent collection dating back to the end of the fifteenth century and containing many priceless treasures. Probably, however, the most valuable gift that possession of the Royal Library brought to the Museum was the right of Copyright deposit, the right to receive a copy of every book published in this country.

With very little money available to buy books the Department grew slowly and the Trustees had to depend largely on the generosity of individual donors. In 1762 came the great collection of pamphlets brought together between 1640 and 1661 by George Thomason, a London bookseller and given to the Department by the young George III. Several other fine collections were received by the end of the century, such as the Garrick plays and the library of the Reverend C. M. Cracherode. In 1819 Sir Joseph Banks bequeathed to the Department his superb collection of books, for the most part of botany, zoology, travel and exploration. In 1828 there came the finest gift the Department has ever received, the magnificent library built up by George III between 1760 and 1820. This was housed in a splendid new gallery, the King's Library, which was designed especially to receive it, and where it still remains.

The Reading Room then consisted of two rooms at the north end of the King's Library, which sufficed until the opening of the present room in 1857. Between 1837 and 1856 Antonio Panizzi, the Keeper of Printed Books, virtually created the modern national library. By securing greatly increased annual grants and by vigorously enforcing the Copyright Act, he succeeded to a large extent in his task of making it the finest in the world.

In 1847, largely through Panizzi's efforts, the Grenville Library was acquired, a collection particularly rich in early printed books. Throughout the later nineteenth century the Department continued to grow in every field. Panizzi designed new book stacks, known as the 'Iron Library', to surround his great circular, domed Reading Room, which were sufficient to contain the ever-expanding library until well into this century.

By the late twenties, however, the question of space was again acute and during the 1930s more extensive stack rooms were constructed to replace the old Iron Library. Before they could be completed, the Second World War broke out, during which one of the remaining quadrants was totally destroyed with the loss of 250,000 books, and the King's Library was badly damaged.

During the course of just over two centuries, the Department has become one of the largest and most comprehensive of all national libraries with a staff of over 700 and containing around 8 million books.

Prints and Drawings

Until 1808 prints and drawings were in a section of the Department of Printed Books. The last Keeper to exercise control over both areas of scholarship was the Reverend William Beloe. He unwittingly reduced the scope of the collection by failing to notice that his friend Robert Dighton, a caricaturist and etcher, was systematically stealing from the Department. It is said that Dighton insinuated himself into the good graces of the easy-going and somewhat *bon vivant* custodian by sending him delicacies for his table. The prints were at that time lightly pasted in guard-books, from which Dighton was able to remove them unnoticed and to carry them away in a portfolio. His thefts were brought to light in 1806 when Samuel Woodburn, the dealer, bought from Dighton an impression of Rembrandt's etching *Landscape with a Coach*. He took it to the Museum to compare it with the example there but of course he found the Museum's impression missing.

As a result of these events the Trustees decided to institute a separate Department of Prints and Drawings and appointed William Alexander as its first Curator. Subsequently, the prints Dighton stole were nearly all recovered and security was tightened.

According to an anonymous pamphlet, the original Print Room was 'in a long narrow room, in the north-east side of Montague House . . . approached by a separate stone staircase, leading to a small vestibule, in the centre of which was the Portland Vase. Passing through a large apartment, appropriated for the Payne Knight and other bronzes, the Print Room was beyond, shut in with a heavy iron door.'

In 1842 the Department went to its second home, in the new Smirke building, but access to the collection was still severely limited. Knight's *Cyclopaedia of London* (1851) says that the Print Room was then housed 'in the north-west angle' among 'collections which are not thrown open to the public generally'.

Material from the Department was first put on display for the public in 1858 and since then there have been countless exhibitions. In 1914 the Department was transferred to its present home in the King Edward VII Building.

Right from the foundation of the Museum in 1752 the prints and drawings have included works of art of major importance, such as Sir Hans Sloane's volume of drawings by Dürer which formed the nucleus of one of the finest collections of that master's work. Subsequent bequests in the early days, notably by the Reverend C. M. Cracherode (some of the finest Rembrandt etchings came from him) and Richard Payne Knight (the splendid series of drawings by Claude Lorrain), enriched the collection. And throughout its long history, further additions by gift, bequest and purchase have resulted in making the Print Room a major centre of the graphic arts in Western Europe, unrivalled for its balanced representation of work by the old masters.

Egyptian Antiquities

Part of the surrender terms of Napoleon's army in Egypt in 1801 was the handing over of some twenty antiquities, including the Rosetta Stone, which he had acquired during his invasion of the country. This was the start of the British Museum's Egyptian collection. In the next two decades the Museum obtained many of its most important sculptures, such as the colossal granite head of Tuthmosis III and the remarkable breccia head of Amenhetes III, just two of the pieces from the private collection of the British Consul-General in Egypt, Henry Salt, which was purchased outright in 1822. From the same collector came most of the Theban tomb paintings which are now in the Third Egyptian Room.

This period marked the beginning of the Museum's collection of Egyptian papyri, which soon received some particularly important additions, notably the group of papyri dating from about 1150 B.C. which record the findings of a commission appointed to investigate robberies of royal tombs in the Theban necropolis and give details of the trials of the thieves. Among other papyri were the Rhine Mathematical Papyrus, the earliest document from Egypt which deals with mathematics, and many literary, magical and religious texts as well.

In 1886, E. A. Wallis Budge, who was later Keeper of the Department, began an important series of visits to Egypt. Each time he brought back objects and papyri of the highest value which enlarged the collection substantially and improved its quality. Among the hundreds of pieces which he acquired, perhaps the outstanding were the limestone statuette of Queen Tetisheri, the Hunters' Palette, the Battlefield Palette and the Eleventh Dynasty historical stela of Tjetji.

The papyri included the Book of the Dead of Ani and the Instructions of Amenemope, some passages in which resemble very closely passages in the Old Testament Book of Proverbs.

Towards the end of the nineteenth century the Egyptian Exploration Society was founded and until the present day its work has been closely associated with the British Museum. Just one small piece, among the countless objects obtained by the Museum from this source, could equal, in any public sale, the amount the Society spends in a year.

Even when the treasures are in this country there is still the problem of preservation. The first week in every month, the entire staff of the Egyptian Department (secretaries as well as scholars) looks over every single object. They are trained to detect any damage or hints of deterioration. Salt is the worst enemy and any soft stone sculpture from a dry climate is likely to have its share. When it is removed from burial under hot sand to the atmosphere of the city it absorbs moisture and could, if not properly treated, explode into powder.

Until 1890 Egyptian antiquities formed part of the Department of Oriental Antiquities, but they were then grouped with those of Western Asia to form the Department of Egyptian and Assyrian Antiquities. This Department existed until 1955 when, largely because of the immense growth in the Western Asiatic collections, it became necessary to divide the antiquities into two separate Departments.

Greek and Roman Antiquities

The British Museum acquired a few Classical antiquities as part of the foundation collection of Sir Hans Sloane, but the first important acquisition was Sir William Hamilton's fine collection of Greek vases and other small antiquities from southern Italy. That was in 1772. A substantial accession of Classical sculpture followed in 1805 with the purchase of Charles Towneley's unrivalled collection of statues, mostly of Roman date.

Greek sculpture came next. The sculptures from the Temple of Apollo at Bassae, near Phigaleia in Arcadia, were acquired in 1815. A year later the collection formed by the Earl of Elgin in Greece in the early years of the nineteenth century was bought for the nation. The greater part of the Elgin Marbles consists of sculptures from the Parthenon in Athens. In 1842–3 a large number of important sculptures, including those from the Harpy Tomb and the Nereid Monument, were excavated for the Museum by Sir Charles Fellows at Xanthus in what is now south-west Turkey. The sculptures from the Mausoleum at near-by Halicarnassus were acquired shortly after, partly by gift from Lord

Stratford de Redcliffe (1846) and partly as a result of the excavations of Sir Charles Newton.

In 1861 the old Department of Antiquities was split into three and Newton became the first Keeper of Greek and Roman Antiquities. The new Department was soon enriched by the arrival of sculptures and architectural ornaments discovered by John Turtle Wood on the site of the great Temple of Artemis (Diana) at Ephesus (1869–74).

The great days of acquisition were now over, and the next major landmark in the history of the Department was the erection of a new gallery for the more spacious display of the sculptures of the Parthenon. Undertaken at the expense of Lord Duveen of Millbank (and known as the Duveen Gallery), it was completed in 1938, but the onset of war in 1939 prevented the installation of the sculptures.

The antiquities of the Greek and Roman Department survived the war intact, but the Department itself suffered considerable bomb damage. The Greek and Roman Life Room and the Bronze Room were destroyed, and the new Duveen Gallery badly damaged.

After the war the collections were gradually reassembled. The sculptures of the Parthenon, at first installed in their pre-war galleries, were finally transferred to their new home, after its repair, in 1962.

This move left three galleries empty on the ground floor, and the opportunity was taken for a complete rearrangement of the departmental collections in a manner more acceptable to modern taste. The ground-floor galleries (the old sculpture galleries) now contain a primary exhibition of sculpture and other antiquities, arranged chronologically, and further reorganization of other galleries is in progress.

Prehistoric and Romano-British Antiquities

It was only in the middle of the nineteenth century that a substantial interest developed in the prehistoric antiquities of Britain and continental Europe. Not until 1850 was a room provided in the British Museum for a display of small British antiquities including prehistoric material, although Romano-British monuments had been assembled on exhibition since 1848. An important step towards the development of the Department of Prehistoric and Romano-British Antiquities was the establishment in 1866 of the Department of British and Medieval Antiquities and Ethnography, with Augustus Wollaston Franks as Keeper.

Ethnography was subsequently separated to form a distinct Department.

By 1877 there were exhibitions in a separate Prehistoric Saloon and a Romano-British Room. The important Roach Smith Collection of Romano-British material from London had been purchased in 1856, and during the next fifty years important acquisitions of prehistoric antiquities came into the Department. There was a greater willingness to spend Museum funds on prehistoric antiquities rather than on more spectacular Greek, Roman, Egyptian or Western Asiatic objects. One of the most notable collections acquired during this period was that of Canon Greenwell, in 1879 and 1909, chiefly remarkable for objects excavated by Greenwell from British barrows. An important collection of Dorset antiquities, including many from the Iron Age hill-fort and Roman fort on Hod Hill, was purchased in 1892 and 1893 from Henry Durden, a grocer in Blandford. Four important continental collections must be mentioned: the Siret Collection of prehistoric Spanish antiquities purchased in 1889, the Klemm Collection of Bronze Age objects from Germany, purchased in 1868, the Edelmann Collection of finds from south Germany, acquired as a gift in 1908, and the Morel Collection containing finds from rich Iron Age burials in north-eastern France, purchased in 1901.

In 1940 the Prehistoric Saloon and Roman British Room were destroyed by bombing, but the collections had been evacuated and were unharmed.

In 1951 a temporary exhibition of prehistoric and Romano-British antiquities was opened in the Roman Britain Room. In the same year there took place the first of eight seasons of excavation at Hod Hill. This was the first major British excavation organized by the British Museum; it was directed by Sir Ian Richmond. Apart from the general desirability of investigating this key site, the excavation provided an archaeological context for the objects from Hod Hill in the Durden Collection.

The planning of the new, permanent exhibition galleries to replace those destroyed in 1940 was associated with the detailed planning of storage accommodation, offices, students' rooms and a workshop for a projected new Department.

On 1 April 1968 the new exhibitions illustrating Prehistoric and Roman Britain were opened to the public, and in April 1969 the Department of British and Medieval Antiquities was divided into two departments, that with later material being named the Department of Medieval and Later Antiquities, and the other, the Department of Prehistoric and Romano-British Antiquities.

Medieval and Later Antiquities

The Department contains antiquities made in Europe from the beginning of the Early Christian era to the twentieth century. In its present form and with its present title, the Department dates back only to 1969, when the Sub-Department of Prehistoric and Romano-British Antiquities was detached from it to become a separate Department on its own and the parent Department was renamed. For the preceding 103 years, it possessed the curiously confusing title of the Department of British and Medieval Antiquities. Its scope extended from the Palaeolithic period to the present day and, until 1921, it also included the Oriental and the Ethnographical collections.

Since its creation in 1866, the Department of British and Medieval Antiquities has had seven Keepers. Perhaps the most remarkable of the seven was Sir Augustus Wollaston Franks, the first of them, and who, for thirty years, formulated the basic policies on which the Department was to develop. His great personal generosity led him to give or to bequeath to the Department many fine collections, such as his silver plate and his jewels and finger-rings, his continental porcelain, in which so many unique signed works have been preserved, or his English pottery, which he offered to give to the Museum in 1887 after the Trustees had authorized him to purchase for the Department all the important pieces in Henry Willett's Collection, in order to make the exhibition more complete. His numerous shrewd purchases on behalf of the Department are, perhaps, overshadowed by his greatest single *coup*, the Royal Gold Cup (*see p. 124*), but it is fitting that another of his brilliant acquisitions, the famous whalebone box, carved in Northumbria in the seventh century A.D., with historical and religious scenes surrounded by runic inscriptions, should be known as 'The Franks Casket'.

Under Franks's successor, Sir Charles Hercules Read, splendid gifts continued to enrich the Department, the most outstanding being the Waddesdon Bequest, a collection of Renaissance *objets d'art* of the finest quality, which Baron Ferdinand Rothschild bequeathed in 1899.

The archaeological interests of the Department were especially fostered under Reginald Smith and Sir Thomas Kendrick. The Department now houses the national collection of archaeological material relating to the Anglo-Saxon and Migration periods, though it was not until 1939 that its greatest excavated treasure, the Sutton Hoo Ship-burial, was discovered and subsequently offered as a gift by the landowner, Mrs E. M. Pretty.

The Department's fine collections of medieval antiquities received a new dimension in 1944 when the Duke of Rutland's vast collection of floor tiles, including several complete pavements, was purchased. Similarly, in 1958 its horological collection became the most important in the world as a result of the acquisition of the famous Ilbert Collection. After Courtney Ilbert's death, his collection of more than 300 clocks was purchased by Mr Gilbert Edgar and presented to the Museum; the watch collection (totalling almost 2000 items) was purchased with funds raised by a public appeal led by the Clockmakers' Company. During the past decade, the Department has been furnished with a fully equipped Horological Students' Room and Library, a technical workshop, and a specialist staff, thereby giving ideal facilities for apprentices, collectors and students to work on this unrivalled concentration of material relating to the history of time-measurement.

Western Asiatic Antiquities

Before A. H. Layard's excavations at the Assyrian sites of Nimrud and Nineveh, the British Museum's collections of Western Asiatic antiquities consisted of little more than a handful of cylinder-seals and cuneiform tablets, and some fragments of sculpture from Persepolis. Layard's excavations from 1845 to 1851 of the sculptured reliefs of the Assyrian palaces aroused great excitement in Victorian England. His work was continued at Nineveh by H. Rassam and W. K. Loftus from 1852 to 1855. In addition to sculptures, these excavators also brought home the great Library of Ashurbanipal, a collection of some 25,000 cuneiform tablets which today forms the cornerstone of Assyriology.

The influx of this material and the need for proper study of the cuneiform inscriptions, eventually successfully deciphered by Colonel Rawlinson, resulted in the formation in 1866 of a separate Department of Oriental Antiquities, and later in the same year a still more specialized Department of Egyptian and Assyrian Antiquities. These Departments were also responsible for the important groups of antiquities being recovered from North Africa, Arabia and Palmyra (Syria).

The renewal of excavations in Mesopotamia, interrupted by the Crimean War, at Nineveh, Balawat, Van (Urartu), and in Babylonia, and purchases made in Baghdad, added tens of thousands of cuneiform tablets to the Museum's collections in addition to several highly important monuments – the Balawat Gates, the Urartian bronze royal throne and the Sun God tablet from Sippar.

The major event of the years between the two world wars was the excavation of Ur by a combined British Museum and University of Pennsylvania team under Sir Leonard Woolley. Their remarkable discovery of the beautiful funerary furniture of the Sumerian Royal Graves aroused world-wide interest; the excavations also yielded a wealth of material illustrating 3000 years of Mesopotamian civilization and important archives of cuneiform tablets.

Since 1945 the primary emphasis has been placed on the proper study, conservation and cataloguing of the collections. In view of the increased speciali-zation needed, the Department of Egyptian and Assyrian Antiquities was split in 1955 into two new Departments, of which the present Department of Western Asiatic Antiquities is responsible for all the pre-Islamic antiquities of the Near East outside Egypt. Since the completion of Woolley's excavations at Tell Atchana, the Museum has ceased to sponsor its own excavations in this area, but has given support to the work of the relevant British Schools of Archaeology, and in particular to the British School of Archaeology in Iraq's excavations at Nimrud. In recent years, the Department has been fully occupied with the rebuilding and rearrangement of its Assyrian Sculpture and other galleries and with the preparation of a large range of catalogues of its collections.

Oriental Antiquities

The Department of Oriental Antiquities was created in 1933. The British Museum already had a considerable collection of works of art from the Far East, south Asia and the Islamic countries of the Near East but hitherto they had been divided among other Departments.

English collectors of Asian art have concentrated mainly on the pottery and porcelain of the Far East. This bias is reflected in the history of the Department, whose first Keeper was R. L. Hobson, probably the greatest scholar in that field. Private collectors, stimulated and often advised by Hobson, give generously to the national collections. The result is the finest display of Chinese ceramics in the world. The collection of early Chinese ritual bronzes is also good and con-tains several masterpieces. Chinese and Japanese painting and sculpture are only fairly represented, with such notable exceptions as the world-famous Ku K'ai Chih scroll and the Stein paintings from central Asia.

As for south Asia, especially India, the English liked only those things which seemed to show Western influence. Hence the collections of Gandhara Buddhist sculpture (first–sixth century A.D.) and of Mughal painting (sixteenth–eighteenth century A.D.) are superlative. Other remarkable acquisitions during the last century include the unique large gilt-bronze Tara from Ceylon in 1830 and the female bracket figure from Sanchi in 1842. The Javanese collection, second only to those in Holland and Java, came from the family of Sir Stamford Raffles. All this would look thin on the ground were it not for the greatest of the Keepers of the British Museum, Augustus Franks, a generous benefactor who was keenly interested in the East. In 1872 the Bridge Collection of Indian sculpture, the finest ever made by a private individual, could not find a bid at auction! Franks persuaded the family to present the whole Collection.

The Islamic collections owe as much to careful purchase as to private generosity. Apart from architecture, the Islamic craftsman lavished all his skill on the so-called 'minor' arts: beautifully written, bound and illustrated books and the objects of everyday. The collection of Persian illustrated manuscripts and paintings is one of the two finest in the world. The pottery is good, the enamelled glass and inlaid metal-work outstanding.

Ethnography

The British Museum has always had an ethnographical element in its exhibitions, for Sir Hans Sloane, one of the Museum's chief benefactors, was an enthusiastic pioneer of what was then the unnamed science of ethnography. The exotic curiosities included especially fine specimens of American and Indian work. Within twenty years of Sir Hans's death, the Pacific had been opened up, and very soon James Cook's discoveries became a major attraction. During the nineteenth century, as the interiors of Africa and South America came within the Department's scope, the collection steadily increased and began to develop the more or less conscious purpose of demonstrating tribal ways of life.

It is this particular purpose that distinguishes the Ethnography Department from other departments. It alone has an anthropological approach to other cultures and it alone seeks to see and present each culture as a whole so that it may be understood in its own terms – in the spirit in which anthropology has been called 'the science of cultural translation'.

However, during the early twentieth century it became more and more difficult, as the number of known cultures increased, to provide a comprehensive account of them all. In fact, by the time it became scientifically possible it was fast becoming practically impossible. At one time, owing to a shortage of storage space, the exhibition bases had to be overfilled to a point at which they approximated to visible storage. The great evacuation at the beginning of the Second World War made it possible to start afresh after the war, and the density of specimens was reduced to about a quarter. But modern standards of exhibition have still further reduced the number of objects with which each of the cultures can be represented. This arrangement at least served the function of drawing attention to the cultures from which the Department had outstanding specimens.

When the Department transferred to its new quarters at the end of 1970 it became clear that the only way in which each tribal culture could be shown comprehensively, while also meeting the demands of modern display standards, was by adding the time dimension to that of space by exhibiting the cultures not simultaneously but serially. So each culture (or each subject) is now on exhibition for about a year before giving place to another, and by 1981 the public should have had an opportunity to see all the Department's major collections. One room is reserved for short-term exhibitions (including loan exhibitions) lasting from three to six months, and another will house some of the principal treasures of the Department whenever they are not otherwise exhibited.

To this programme of exhibitions much of the Department's other important activities are geared, from the publications which accompany each display, to the work of the conservation section in preparing and restoring objects for exhibition – not to mention the fieldwork that supplements the collections from a particular culture. The anthropological approach which makes well-rounded wholes of all these exhibitions also makes them a useful introduction to the other departments of the British Museum.

Manuscripts

Proposals for the establishment of a national collection of manuscripts can be traced back to the sixteenth century, when English scholars began to appreciate their outstanding historical value. A unique opportunity was provided by the dispersal of the monastic libraries after the Dissolution, but attempts to interest successive Tudor sovereigns in the idea failed. It was left to antiquaries such as Sir Robert Cotton (1571–1631) to save what they could from the wreck. Of all the private libraries so formed, that of Cotton, who had a passionate interest in British history, was the finest, and it was freely accessible to scholars. In 1700, his grandson presented it to the nation. But the setting up of a national collection had to wait until 1753, when the death of Sir Hans Sloane provided the opportunity of using as a nucleus his extensive library and vast natural history collections. When the British Museum was created, it embodied the Sloane and Cotton collections, together with the great Harley collection of manuscripts bought at the same time; a few years later, George II added the manuscripts and printed books in the Royal Library.

The Museum originally consisted of only three Departments, Manuscripts, Printed Books, and Natural and Artificial Productions. From the latter have developed the various Departments of Antiquities in the British Museum, together with the whole of the Natural History Museum. The Departments of

Manuscripts and of Printed Books, on the other hand, have survived almost unaltered, though each has surrendered its Oriental material to the Department of Oriental Printed Books and Manuscripts.

During its 218 years of existence, the Department's collections have steadily grown, standards of cataloguing have been established and constantly improved, and there has been a constant expansion in the various services offered to the public, whether through direct consultation of manuscripts in the Students' Room, the supply of photographs and microfilms or a vast and ever-increasing correspondence. Despite these changes, a basic continuity is evident. The scope of the Department covers, as it has for so long, handwritten material of all kinds in Western languages – an all-embracing definition which includes, for instance, manuscript music, manuscript maps and topographical drawings, while art is represented by its world-famous collection of medieval illuminated manuscripts. From the beginning, moreover, the outlook of the Department has been international, and although the emphasis is necessarily upon the art, history and literature of the British Isles, those of other countries and cultures are not neglected.

Severely restricted in space, and lacking custom-built premises and fittings, the Department is rapidly approaching the limit of what it can achieve in its present surroundings. It now stands on the threshold of a new era – its incorporation as a unit in the projected British Library, with the possibilities of expanding and improving its collections and services on an unprecedented scale. This prospect of achieving its destiny as the National Manuscript Collection is at once its greatest challenge and its greatest opportunity.

Coins and Medals

The Department of Coins and Medals has existed as an independent section of the Museum since 1861. Before then its collections belonged first to the Department of Manuscripts and subsequently to Antiquities. It is one of the most important of such collections in the world, consisting of nearly three-quarters of a million specimens from all countries and periods. Coinage had no antecedents in Egypt or Babylonia, but the main stream began with ancient Greece, spreading out to other peoples such as the Persians, Phoenicians, Arabians and Celts, and – most importantly – to Rome, from whose Imperial coinage there evolved the coinage tradition of medieval Europe which was further developed in modern times to spread over the whole world. There were quite separate traditions in ancient China and India, while in the seventh century A.D. the Islamic world originated yet another. The Museum's collection covers all these fields comprehensively, and has a further important element in the collection of portrait and commemorative medals from the Italian Renaissance to the present day.

The basis of the collection was laid down in the eighteenth century by the Cotton and Sloane Cabinets, to which were added those of Cracherode (1799), the Banks sisters (1818), the Royal Collection presented to the nation by King George IV in 1823 and the brilliant Greek Collection of Richard Payne Knight (1824). The process has continued with accessions of Roman coins from Count de Salis and Edward Wigan; and the Oriental and especially the Indian sections were built up by the India Office Collection (1882) and that of General Cunningham (1893). The Bank of England Collection considerably augmented the series of British coins in 1877, and that of Edward Hawkins the British medals. Outstanding twentieth-century accessions include the donation by Sir Arthur Evans of his father's Celtic coins, the Seager and Mavrogordato Bequests, and the important Lloyd Bequest of Greek coins of Sicily and Italy. The Clarke-Thornhill Bequest vastly extended the holdings of continental European coinage. Purchases from treasure trove have also made very significant contributions – for instance the Roman gold hoard from Bredgar (1957) and the huge silver hoard from Dorchester (1936); and a number of notable hoards, such as those from Cuerdale, Chester, Tealby, and recently Colchester, form a very large element in the English medieval section. Numerous gifts and purchases ensure the constant growth and ever-increasing comprehensiveness of the collection.

The entire contents of the Department were removed from London for safety during the Second World War – fortunately indeed, since the empty premises were bombed in 1941 and only restored in 1959. The Department still lacks the space to exhibit its treasures to the public. On the other hand, every year as many as 5000 students and inquirers visit the Department, which constitutes one of the foremost centres of numismatic knowledge and research.

Biographical Notes

MICHAEL AYRTON is a painter, sculptor, author, theatrical designer and illustrator. He has exhibited in many galleries in Britain and the United States, written several books and many articles about his own and other people's art and is a frequent broadcaster.

SIR JOHN BETJEMAN, the poet and author, was awarded the CBE in 1960, made a C.Lit. in 1968 and knighted in 1969. In addition to his literary reputation he is known as a leading campaigner for the preservation of Victorian architecture. He is a frequent broadcaster.

ASA BRIGGS is Professor of History and Vice-Chancellor of the University of Sussex. Formerly Fellow of Worcester College, Oxford (1945–55), and Professor of Modern History, University of Leeds (1955–61). Author of many books on nineteenth- and twentieth-century history, including his famous three-volume history of broadcasting in the UK. Professor Briggs appears frequently on radio and television. He is a Governor of the British Film Institute.

FLEUR COWLES is a painter and writer. She was Associate Editor of *Look* for over ten years and launched her own magazine, *Flair*. She has written three books and is at present preparing a fourth; her paintings have been exhibited in London, New York and several of the major European cities. Fleur Cowles was born in the United States but lives in London when she is not on one of her many travels abroad.

ROBERT ERSKINE was born in London in 1930 and lived in India as a child. Studied prehistoric archaeology at Cambridge. In 1955 he opened the St George's Gallery as a pioneer centre for modern artists, and since that date has broadcast regularly on television on subjects such as the theme of his contribution to this book. He has also made films for television on ancient India, Persia, Egypt and North Africa. He is now writing a large television series on the Roman Empire.

LADY ANTONIA FRASER is the eldest daughter of the Earl and Countess of Longford. Her biography of Mary Queen of Scots won the James Tait Black Memorial Prize and is an international best-seller. She also writes on children's subjects, and appears on television. She is currently working on a biography of Oliver Cromwell. Lady Antonia is married and has six children.

SIR TYRONE GUTHRIE's career in the theatre extended over several countries with productions in the United States, Australia, Finland and Israel. He was Director of the Old Vic in the early 1950s and founded the Tyrone Guthrie Theatre, Minneapolis and the Stratford Theatre, Ontario. Sir Tyrone died in May 1971 at the age of seventy.

JOHN HALE is Professor of Italian at University College, London. He was formerly Fellow and Tutor in Modern History at Jesus College, Oxford, Professor of History at the University of Warwick and Visiting Professor of History at the Berkeley campus of the University of California. Most of his books and articles have been devoted to the Italian Renaissance. His latest book is *Renaissance Europe* in Collins Fontana paperback History of Europe. He is forty-seven, married and lives in Twickenham.

THE RT HON. MALCOLM MACDONALD, OM, PC, is an experienced statesman and has travelled widely in the Far East, Asia, Africa and Canada. Hon. Fellow of Queen's College, Oxford, and honoured by the universities of Hanoi, Hong Kong, Singapore and Malaya. Has held numerous posts, including Special Representative of HM Government in a number of Commonwealth countries in East and Central Asia; British High Commissioner, Governor-General, Governor and Commander-in-Chief, Kenya; UK High Commissioner in Canada; Secretary of State for the Colonies and for Dominion Affairs; Governor-General of Malaya and British Borneo; High Commissioner in India; Commissioner-General for the UK in South-East Asia; and UK representative on the South-East Asia Treaty Council.

J. E. MORPURGO, Professor of American Literature in the University of Leeds, was born in London in 1918 and educated at Christ's Hospital and the College of William and Mary in Virginia. He was for many years associated with Penguin Books and from 1954 to 1969 was Director-General of the National Book League. His publications include *The Pelican History of the United States* (with R. B. Nye), editions of the works of Charles Lamb, Leigh Hunt and Fenimore Cooper, and several travel books among them *American Excursion, The Road to Athens* and *Venice*. His most recent book is a life of Sir Barnes Wallis.

DR DAVID STAFFORD-CLARK is Physician in Charge, Department of Psychological Medicine, Director of the York Clinic, Guy's Hospital, London. He has held numerous medical posts, and is the author of two collections of poetry and various works of non-fiction.

GWYN THOMAS was born in the Rhondda Valley and is the son of a miner. Educated at Porth Grammar School and, on scholarships, at the Universities of Oxford and Madrid. Professions: teaching, lecturing, and writing novels and plays, flanked by much work on radio and television. Attributes his interest in the Romano-British to a teacher obsessed by a love for the memory of Boadicea, Queen of the Iceni, and hatred for Suetonius Paulinus, who killed her.

SIR JOHN WOLFENDEN is Director and Principal Librarian of the British Museum. Educated at Wakefield School, Queen's College, Oxford, and Princeton University, USA, Sir John has followed a distinguished career in education. He was Headmaster of Uppingham School, then Shrewsbury School, before becoming Vice-Chancellor of Reading University. He holds honorary degrees from Hull and Reading Universities. He has served on a number of advisory and Government committees with special reference to young people and education. A lecturer and writer, his works include *The Approach to Philosophy* and *Education in a Changing World*.

BRIGADIER PETER YOUNG (rtd), DSO, MC, commanded the 9th Regiment of the Arab Legion from 1953 to 1956, holds the Order of El Istiglal of Jordan, and is fluent in Arabic. He was Editor of Purnell's *History of the First World War* and of *Decisive Battles of the Second World War* (1967). Lecturer in Military History, Royal Academy of Sandhurst (1959–69). Commander of No. 3 Commando (1943–4) and 1st Commando Brigade (1945–6). MC 1942 and two bars 1943.